地產營銷空間

样板房·售楼处·酒店

MARKETING SPACE REAL ESTATE

Y·L·H 室内设计作品

張雲 張浪 張怀 著

中国轻工业出版社
全国百佳图书出版单位

雲 The source of the design: innovative ideas of Clouds and Fall papers

烟落紙的創意是設計之源

设计师的创意，不是简单的破陈除旧，更不是一味地求新立异。创意，常常来自设计师的灵感乍现，但它更来自设计师对项目立意的深入理解，对环境空间的整体把握。好的创意，无处可寻，却又无处不在；它是贯穿整个项目的灵魂，是一个好作品得以脱胎的源泉——就像高超玄妙的书法，挥毫间逸兴横飞，如同云烟一样变幻莫测、美妙多姿；待笔墨落纸，你就会发现，布局谋篇、起承转合，处处有迹可循，处处体现了作者独特的匠心。

The designers' ideas, is not a simple way of giving up the old issues, and not a way of pursuing new and different things. Creation, often comes from the inspiration of the designer, but it also sourced from the deep understanding of the project ideas for the designers, and the whole glimpse of the whole space. A good idea, nowhere to be found, but everywhere; it is the soul of the whole project, it is a good artwork, which was like the great mystery of calligraphy; in the whole, it was like unpredictable and wonderful clouds, for the ink and paper, you will find, organizing the handling down, there are telltale signs everywhere, and everywhere was embodied the author's unique craftmanship.

浪里淘沙的追求是設計之本

The soul of the design: waves in the pursuit of Taosha

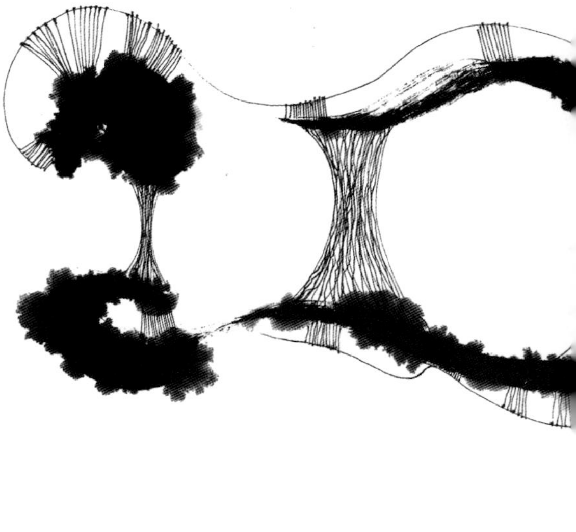

我们的理想，是希望我们打造的每一个作品，能够让身处其中的每一个人都体验到快乐。为此，我们不断地挑战，不断地突破。取色彩变化，用线条肌理，采灯影光晕，凭物器摆设，跨越古典与现代，契合奢华与简约。不是没有遭遇瓶颈，也曾面临困境，但人文情怀的设计梦想，赋予了我们力量和信念。我们坚信，一个好作品，能受得住人们的评判，经得起时间的考验。时光淌过流年，铅华洗尽的，会是经典。

Our ideal, expect us to make every effort to make you a masterpiece, which can let everyone in space, experience the happy mood. To this end, we constantly challenge, constantly breakthroughs. Images in color changes, with line texture, adopt the halo, with content in decoration, crossing the classical and modern style, with luxury and contracted factors. Not a bottleneck and face difficulties, but the design of the humanity dreams, gives us strength and conviction. We firmly believe that a good work can live the good people of the judge, stand the test of the time. Time offered a year, it is still the Classic work of design.

Contents 目录

BEIJING GUANSHANYUE B AGAINST VILLA MODEL HOUSES

北京观山悦B反别墅样板房

Project name: Beijing Guanshanyue B against Villa model houses
Developer: Beijing Tech-Park Construction (Group) Ltd
Construction area: 450 square meters
Using material: grey wood stone, brilliantly coloured purple stone, oak veneer, senior wallpaper, leather, metal, carve patterns or designed on woodwork, singeing brown stone, deep Hang stone, Grey Coloured glass, manual coloured drawing or pattern, senior paint, senior real wood floor
Project location: Beijing
Design time: March, 2012

项目名称： 北京观山悦B反别墅样板房
开发商： 北京科技园建设(集团)股份有限公司
建筑面积： 450m^2
使用物料： 灰木纹石材、幻彩紫石材、橡木饰面、高级壁纸、皮革、金属雕花、烧毛石材、深杭啡石材、灰茶镜、手工彩绘、高级涂料、高级实木地板
项目地点： 北京
设计时间： 2012年3月

观山悦地理位置得天独厚，北观山景，南沐阳光。本案是面积450多平方米的大户型别墅样板房。设计师以深厚的中国文化为底蕴，融入现代化的创意，使整个空间在沉稳内敛的中式外表下，不乏温婉纤丽的点缀，呈现出优雅的高贵气质。

餐厅使用了木纹石材铺贴造型，结合深色木饰面金属圈边，古朴而不失时尚。

走廊及过道的创意取自中国传统的窗格式拼花。在设计师的精心排列下，抽象的花型，一路优雅地绽放，给每一个步入别墅的人带来轻松愉快的心情。

客厅以深咖色为主，搭着暗灰与茶色，诠释了中式风的庄重典雅。花格配上镜面，则让整个空间的线条变得生动。浅色的地面，金色的靠枕，为原本沉稳的客厅增添了几分跳跃的生机，既表现了迎宾待客的欢喜，又凸显了其高雅的生活格调。

书房的设计是本案的点睛之笔。在这里，设计师摈弃了复杂的造型。一整块硬木加工而成的书桌，充满质感；用木纹石材和旧木饰面组合而成的储物格，古朴安静；加上一整面落地玻璃的设计，整个书房显得简洁、大气；青瓷筒和展开的画卷，散发着独特的人文内涵及艺术气息。在这里，静可品茗阅读，动则挥毫泼墨，无不尽情尽兴。

楼梯护栏采用镂空的方式，原创的中式窗格拼花再次点缀其间，和走廊、过道遥相呼应。吊顶上的手绘图案，轻柔舒展，姿态美丽。放眼望去，整个空间动中有静，刚柔并济。

Guanshanyue has advantageous geographical location, north next to mountain, south to soak up the sun. This case is an area of 450 square meters large family villa example. The designer with profound Chinese culture as the background, into the modern ideas, under the Chinese style appearance of composed inside collection, there is no lack of beautiful center ornament, appear elegant noble temperature.

Restaurant to use the old blue brick files in the modeling of the shop is stuck, combined with dark wood veneer metal circle edge, of primitive simplicity and do not break vogue.

Corridor and the creative aisle spelling a flower from the window of Chinese traditional format. Under the careful arrangement of the designer the abstract pattern, elegant bloom all the way, in this way, everyone who comes to the villa can have a pleasant and comfortable mood.

The sitting room is given priority with the deep coffee color, a dark grey and dark brown, explained the Chinese tradition of grave and elegant. Beautiful case with mirror, let the whole space line becomes vivid. The ground of the light color, golden pillows, as originally composed of the sitting room, which added a few minutes of jumping to life, both shows the joy, welcome guests and highlights the elegant life style.

The design of the study is the nods eyeball pen of the case. Here, the designer gives up complex modeling. The desk was made up by a piece of hardwood, full of simple sense, used for old blue bricks and wood veneer combination storage, with primitive simplicity and quiet environment; Plus a whole born glass surface design, the whole study room appears concise and atmospheric, Celadon tube and a scroll, sending out the unique cultural connotation and artistic breath. Here, being in a quiet environment, you can read based on a cup of tea, being in a moving state with her, all happiness will be around.

Stair railing was adopted by the hollow out, and the original Chinese window flower was used for dotting in the zoom, and in comparison with the corridors and aisles. And the hand-painted design on the ceiling, gently stretch, beautiful look, the whole space was combined with the static and moving states, which seems better for the whole environment.

负一层平面布置图

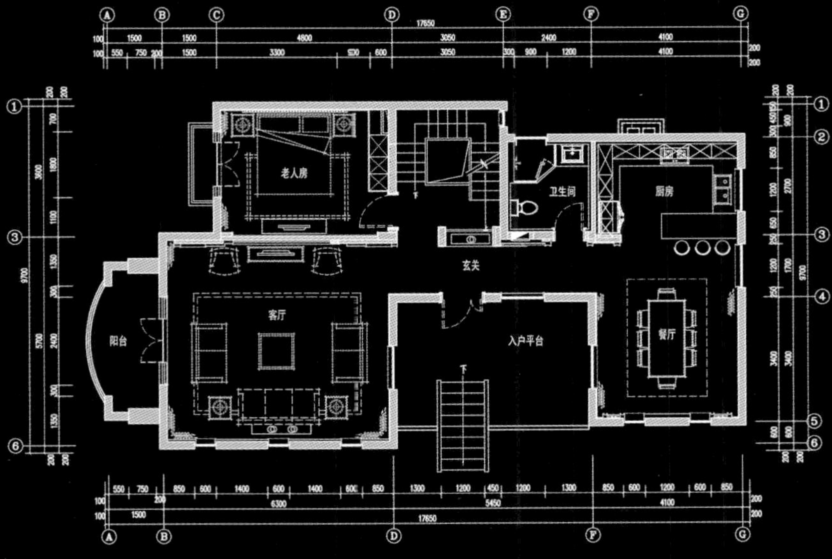

一层平面布置图

二层平面布置图

本草綱目
Secretele medicinei alternative
BOSCH

CINDERELLA

02

YORKSHIRE COUNTY NEW CLASSIC MODEL HOUSES IN CHONGQING CITY

重庆约克郡新古典样板房

Project name: Yorkshire County New Classic Model houses in Chongqing city
Developer: Hongkong Land Holding Co.Ltd.
Construction area: 450 square meters
Using materials: New cream-colored stone, grey wood stone, light brown stone, senior wallpaper, leather, computer carved patterns, designed patterns on the woodwork, black mirror, ebony veneer, senior paintings, senior real wood floor board
Location of project: Chongqing
Design time: August, 2011

项目名称： 重庆约克郡新古典样板房
开发商： 香港置地控股有限公司
建筑面积： 450m^2
使用物料： 新西米黄石材、灰木纹石材、浅啡网石材、高级壁纸、皮革、电脑雕刻雕花、深杭啡石材、黑镜、黑檀木饰面、高级涂料、高级实木复合地板
项目地点： 重庆
设计时间： 2011年8月

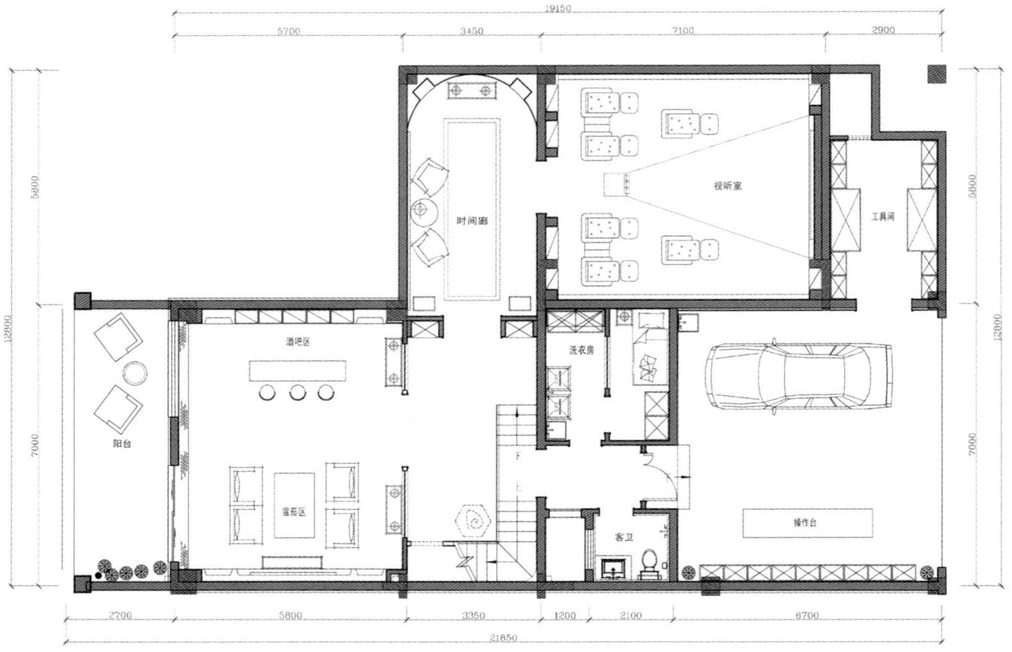

负一层平面布置图

本案项目位于重庆两江新区核心地带，背靠照母山森林公园，面临重光水库，自然环境十分优越。设计师充分考虑到项目的地理位置、客户群体和户型特点，在样板房的打造中突出了优雅独特、华丽出众的新古典主义风格。

在颜色搭配上，设计师巧妙运用了黑钢与浅咖色的对比，理性中透着灵气。在装饰方面，则大胆使用银镜和金属元素，使空间通透明亮，实现了古典与现代的完美结合。

客厅、卧室和书房大面积铺陈了米黄色的石材和浅色的壁纸，加上暖色的灯光，温馨感油然而生。精心挑选的艺术摆件，彰显高雅品位。彩色的靠枕，美丽的鲜花，使得空间更加生动，营造出轻松浪漫的氛围。

餐厅的大面积落地窗户，挂上轻质透光的纱窗，阳光倾洒进来，外景绿植隐约呈现，令人心情大好，食欲倍增。设计师在追求美感的同时，充分考虑了人的心理，秉承了功能至上的宗旨。

The project is located in the central area of Chongqing Liangjiang new districts,back against the Forest Park, facing Chongguang reservoir, so the natural environment is extremely advantageous. Designers consider all the factors in the projects, including the location of the project, customers groups and also the characteristics of the family, in the model housing, to highlight the elegant and unique, neoclassical style.

In terms of the color allocation, designer combined the black steel and light coffee color, and also compared among them, which show the spirit among rational ideology. From the point of the decoration, to use boldly silver mirror and metal element, make the space connected fully bright, and to realize the perfect combination of the classical and modern factors.

Sitting room, bedroom and study room were put the beige stone and light color wallpaper, plus the warm color light, human beings will have sweet feeling in his/her mind spontaneously. The art of carefully selected furnished artworks, to show a sense of elegant. Colorful pillows, beautiful flowers, to make the space more lively, build a relaxed and romantic atmosphere.

The restaurant's large area ground impact window, hang up the light transmittance of screen window, the sunshine shed come in, to see outside, exterior green plant looming, people will have a good mood from this scenery and at the same time, will have appetite doubled. The senior designer is not only in the process of pursuing the sense of the beauty in the model houses, but also take full consideration of the person's psychology adhering to the core principle of the function of design.

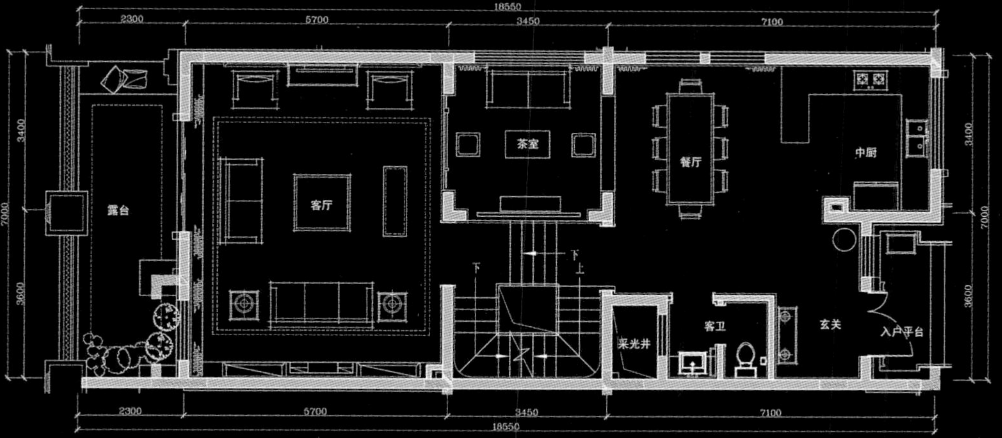

首层平面布置图

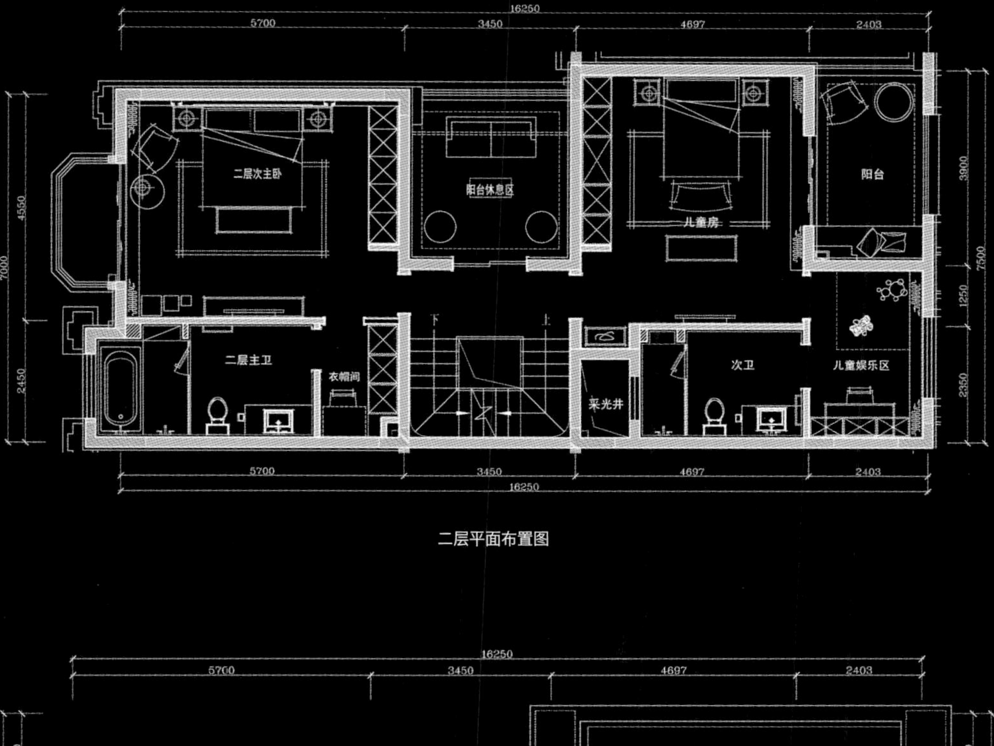

二层平面布置图

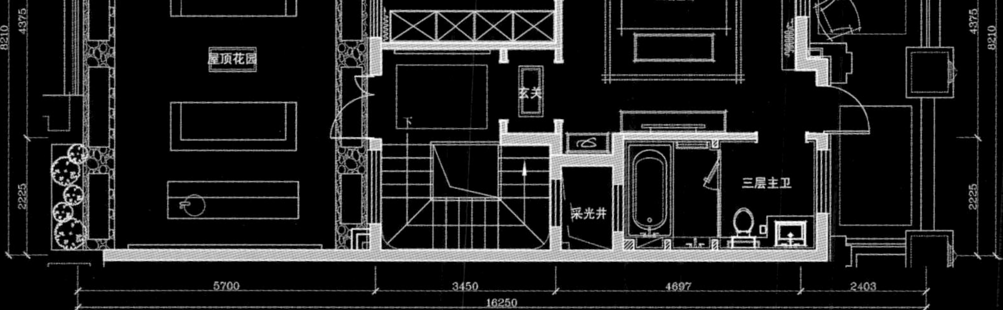

三层平面布置图

NO.0712

VINCI
BROWN

HOLLYWOOD
CHAPTERS
SET UP
EXTRAS
HOW TO

TOTO

03

TANGSHAN BOYUESHAN BUILDING SALES OFFICE

唐山铂悦山售楼处

Project name: Tangshan Boyueshan Building Sales Office
Developer: Longji Taihe Real estate co.Ltd.
Construction area: 2000 square meters
Using materials: Guizhou wood stone, Xixili materials, light brown network, new cream-colored stone, senior wallpaper, leather, black and white roots, mirror stainless stone, rose-stained on the golden paintings
Location of the project: Tangshan city
Design time: In February, 2013

项目名称： 唐山铂悦山售楼处
开发商： 隆基泰和实业有限公司
建筑面积： 2000 m^2
使用物料： 贵州木纹石材、西西里灰、浅啡网、新西米黄石材、高级壁纸、皮革、黑白根、镜面不锈钢、玫瑰金
项目地点： 河北唐山
设计时间： 2013年2月

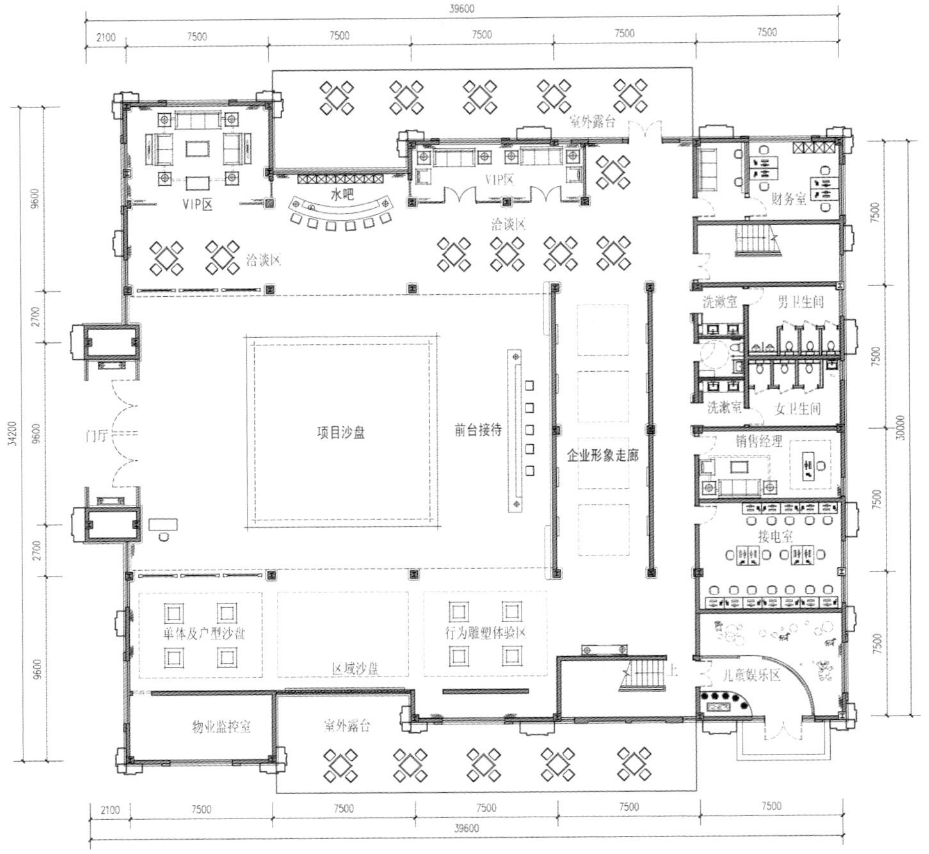

首层平面-平面图

售楼处作为业主走近项目的第一站，除了满足洽谈签约的功能，也是体验优异居住文化的媒介。本案的设计，处处考虑人与空间的关系，融合东方哲学思想与西式空间风格，赋予整个接待空间新的内涵，让访客的到来仿佛与空间融为一体。售楼处的设计重点，不以空间尺度或量体规模取胜，而更注重细致的光影效果、线条切割与材质变化，灌注出美轮美奂的细节享受。

售楼处接待大厅顶部三层叠级玫瑰金圈吊，内部打上灯带，自然而然成为视觉焦点。天花顶面则用黑镜钢雕花，实现了光和亮面材质的完美结合，鲜明地展现了售楼处的主题元素。

洽谈区的玫瑰金屏风，菱形挖空处理，创造性地与天花吊顶主题元素相呼应，同时也成为视线与光线的沟通管道。各立面以细致的建材变化与金属线条的沟刻，分割重组间创造出光影轨迹，在反射和穿透中展现出多样性层次，在虚实镂空间流露出华丽的时尚感。

The sales office is regarded as the first stop of the project for the approaching owners, apart from satisfying discuss signing functions, also as a medium of experiencing the excellent residential culture. The design of the case, everywhere to consider the relationship between human and space, to integrate the eastern philosophy and western space style, and put new sense of the space in the process of reception, let the arrivers experience the integration with the space. The core design point in the sales department, not won by spatial scale or quantity body size, and pay more attention to the light and shadow of a careful, line cutting and material changes, filling out the details of the beautiful enjoyment.

The sales office, there are three level cascade rose-golden ring in the reception hall, internal wall was put with lamp belt, so naturally become the visual focus. The ceiling was made by the black steel flowers, to realize the perfect combination of the light and bright, to the show unique factor of the sales office.

The Discussion area was used by the rose-golden screen, a hollowed out diamond processing, innovatively to match the themes of smallpox condole, and also become the line of sight communication channel with light. The facade with meticulous building materials change and the metal line groove, split between restructuring to create the light track, and to show the diversified and transmissional levels in the reflection, and lead to the luxuriant and fashionable feeling in the actual and hollow space situation.

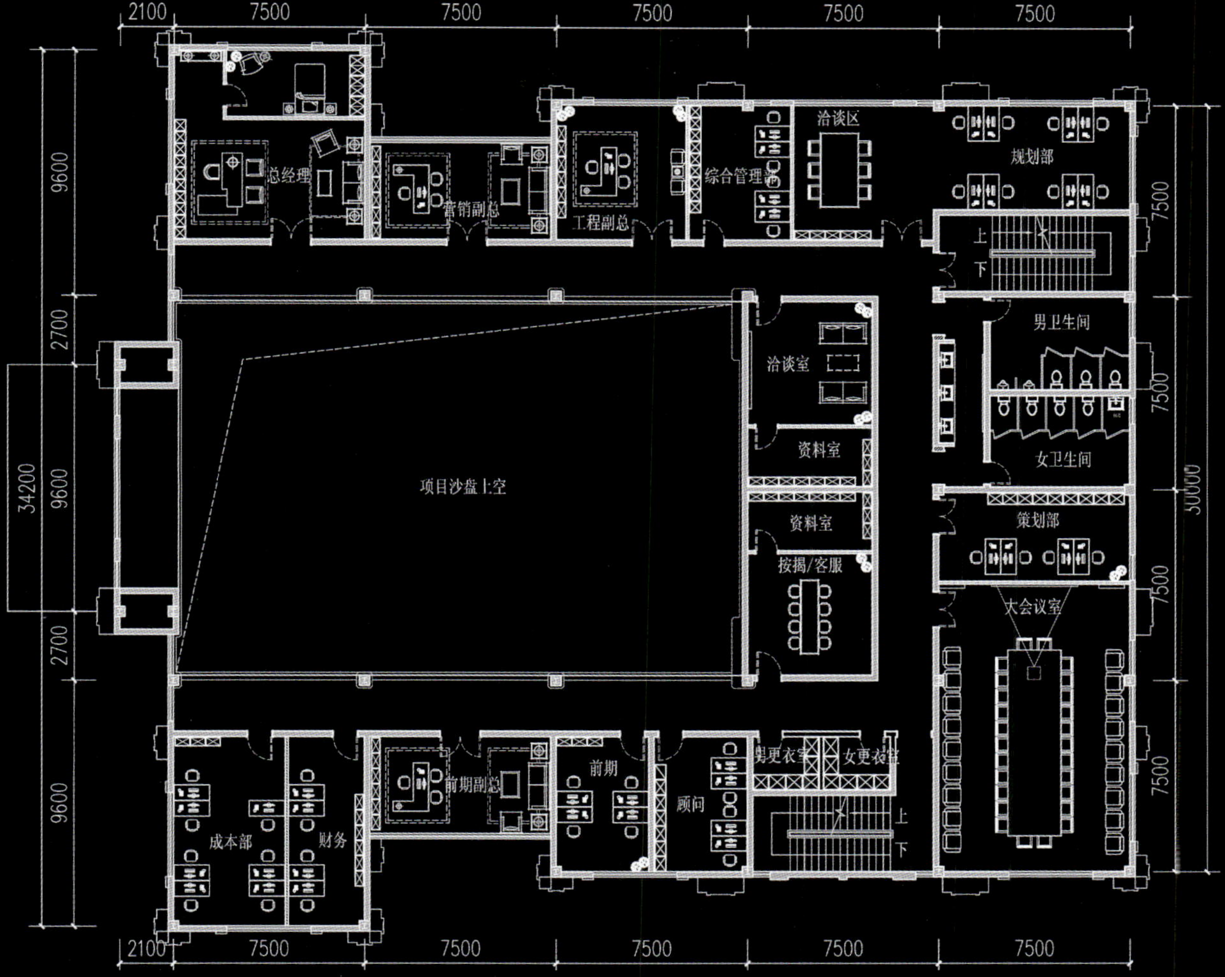
2100
7500
7500
7500
7500
7500
9600
2700
9600
2700
9600
34200
7500
7500
7500
7500
30000
总经理
营销副总
工程副总
综合管理部
洽谈区
规划部
上
下
男卫生间
女卫生间
洽谈室
资料室
资料室
按揭/客服
项目沙盘上空
策划部
大会议室
成本部
财务
前期副总
前期
顾问
男更衣室
女更衣室
上
下

二层平面-平面布置图

04

YORKSHIRE COUNTY VILLA ENGLAND STYLE MODEL HOUSES IN CHONGQING CITY

重庆约克郡别墅英伦样板房

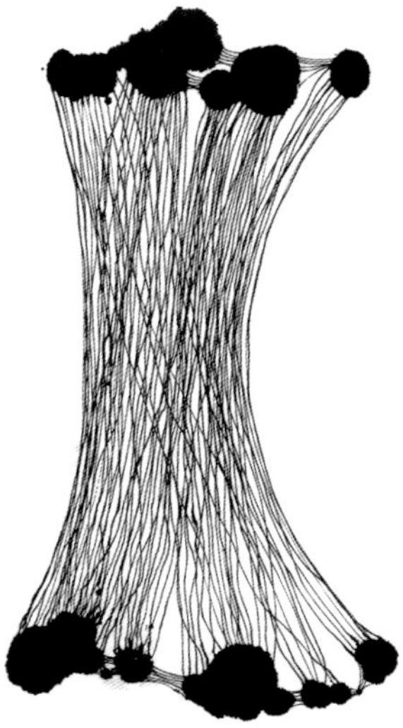

Project name: Yorkshire County Villa England Style Model Houses in Chongqing City
Developer: Hongkong Land Holding co.Ltd
Construction area: 480 square meters
Using materials: new cream-colored stone, stone circle line, flannelette hard package, senior wallpaper, leather, yellow carve stone, black golden flowers, tropical rain forest, ebony stone veneer, senior coatings, high real wood joint floor board
Location of the project: Chongqing
Design time: in June, 2011

项目名称： 重庆约克郡别墅英伦样板房
开发商： 香港置地控股有限公司
建筑面积： 480 m^2
使用物料： 新西米黄石材、石材圈线、绒布硬包、高级壁纸、皮革、黄洞石、黑金花石材、热带雨林、黑檀木饰面、高级涂料、高级实木复合地板
项目地点： 重庆
设计时间： 2011年6月

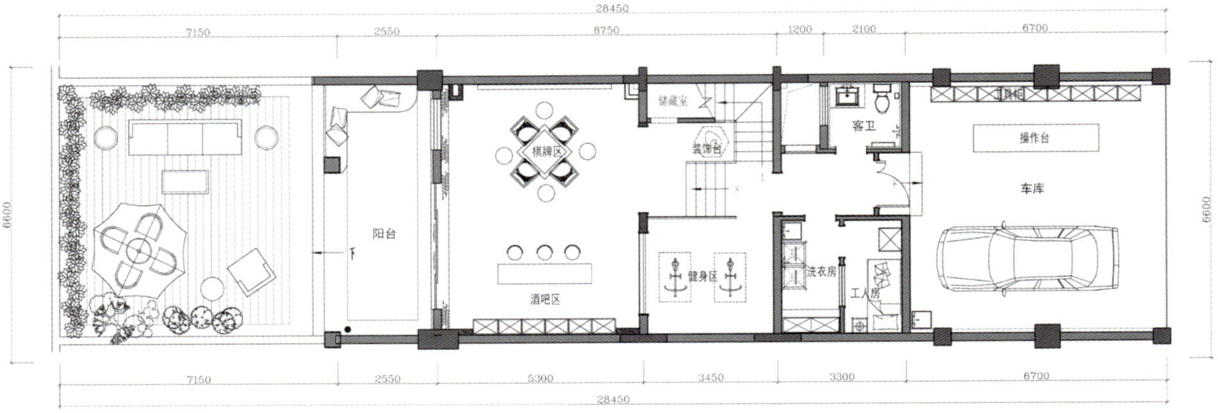

负一层平面布置图

约克郡是重庆高端项目的代表。而样板间无疑是高端客户的向导。尊贵优雅、含蓄自然的英伦风，成为本案设计师的首选。

雍容华丽的色彩，格子与条纹，深色的家具，有故事感的沙发，古朴中透出一丝丝尊贵。蓝色沙发，紫红色的印花地毯，做工精细的摆件，则散发着浓郁的贵族气息。

过道的线条简洁明快，一气呵成。再忙碌的人到这里后，步伐也会变得从容。一个个静谧而又明媚的房间，透露着一种没有任何杂念的朴实。唯美的傍晚，余晖透过纱窗，拉出长长的影子，洒落一室的斑斓，令人忍不住心动、驻足，久久停留。

Yorkshire County is a representative of Chongqing high-end projects. And the model houses are the guide of the high-end customers. Noble and elegant, reserved, natural style of England, and became the first choice of the unique designer.

Grace and gorgeous color, grid and stripe, brunet furniture, the sofa with a sense of story, a touch of primitive simplicity and honor. The printing of the blue sofa, purple carpet, fine workmanship of furnishing artworks, which sends out the rich aristocratic breath.

Aisle, line is concise and lively. For the very busy people, the pace of them will keep calm. Each room is quiet and beautiful, disclose a kind of simplicity. Beautiful evening light through the window screen, pull long shadow on the colors of one room, people who approach it cannot help but move in their mind, stop, and keep calm for a long time at that place.

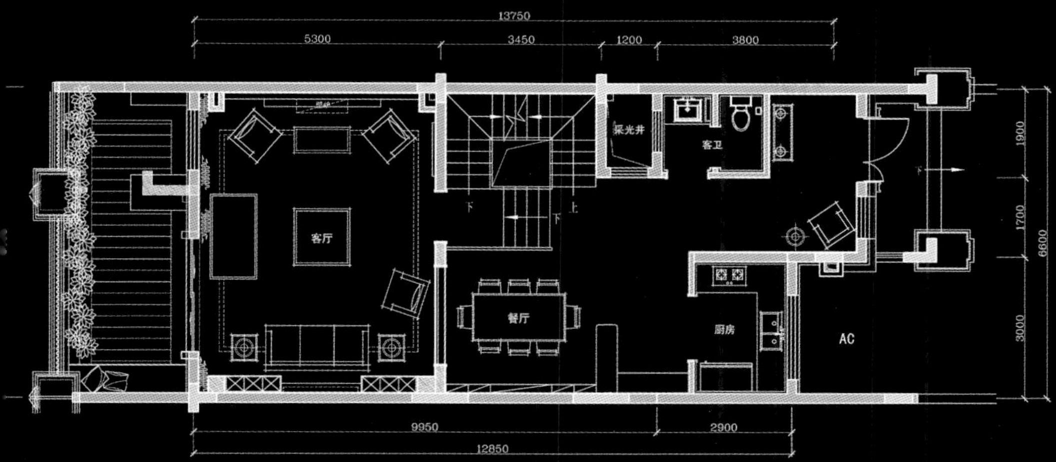

一层平面布置图

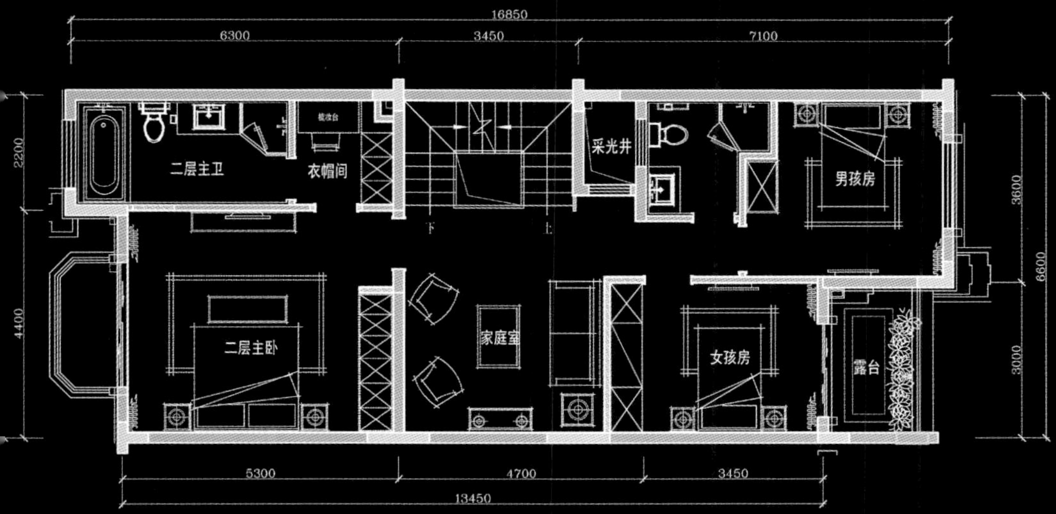

二层平面布置图

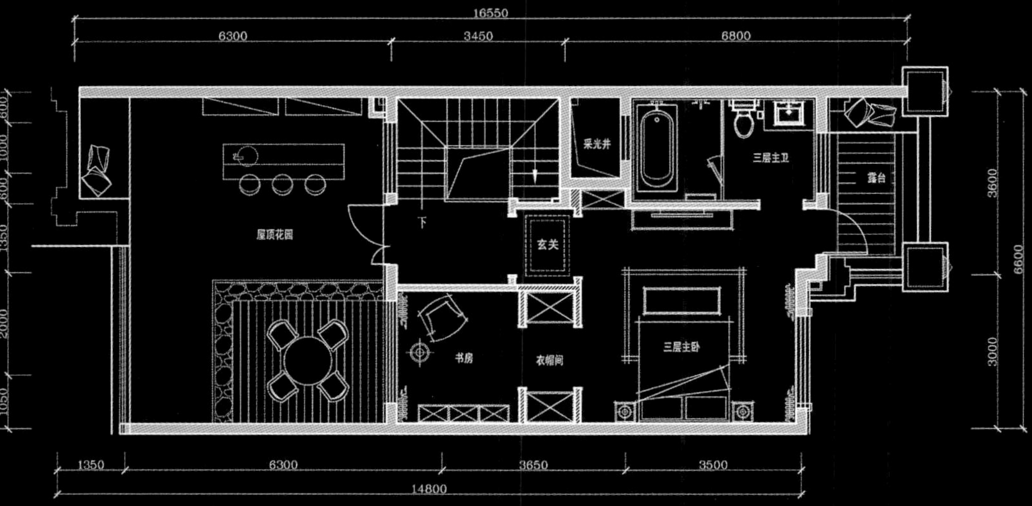

三层平面布置图

流连于湖，醉心斜风细雨不须归的悠然

Frequently asked questions

AK-47

05

CHANGJIAHUI E MODEL HOUSES IN CHONGQING CITY

重庆长嘉汇E户型样板间

Project name: Changjiahui E Model houses in Chongqing city
Developer: Hongkong Land & Investment real estate developers
Construction area: 98 square meters
Using materials: Grey wood, senior wallpaper, leather, senior deep brown, peirce white stone, black mirror, ebony veneer, senior coatings, high solid real wood floor board
Location of project: Chongqing
Design time: In January, 2012

项目名称： 重庆长嘉汇E户型样板间
开发商： 香港置地&招商地产
建筑面积： 98 m^2
使用物料： 灰木纹石材、高级壁纸、皮革、深杭啡、雅士白石材、黑镜、黑檀木饰面、高级涂料、高级实木复合地板
项目地点： 重庆
设计时间： 2012年1月

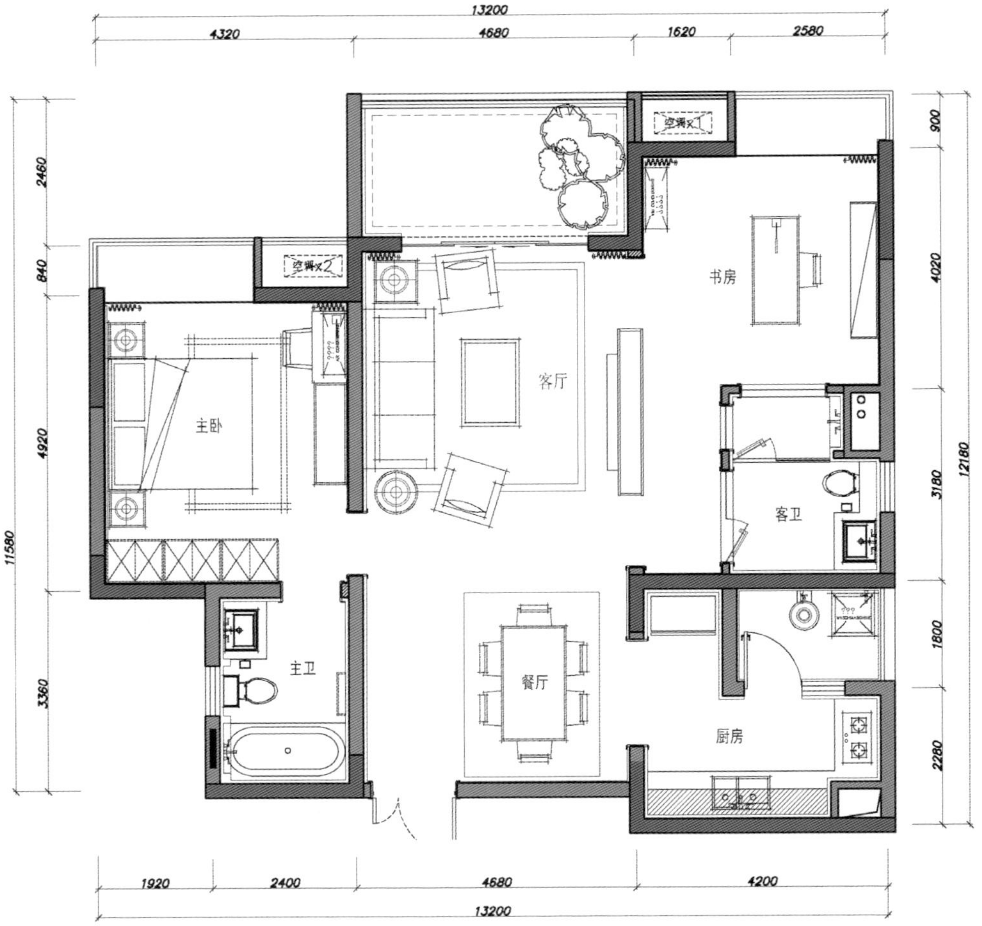

当时尚撞上古典，当优雅遇上阳刚，会产生一种怎样的效果？这个空间正好向我们诠释了一种这样的生活态度：不媚俗、不一味迎合潮流，坚持自己独特的品位，追寻浓郁的文化，崇尚优雅的生活。

客厅电视墙用四大片银狐大理石拼成，厚实利落，极具质感，让整个客厅透出传统的韵味。一组黑色的真皮沙发，稳重又奢华。沙发的硬包排列和黑镜的组合，加上现代科技感的金属雕塑端景，为空间注入浪漫色彩，并和餐厅的主色调相互对应。而客、餐厅走道三处主要端景面，以淡雅的进口涂料展现。利落的玻璃镜面展示柜，在黑镜钢反射光源下，陈列的艺术品尽显卓然品位。事实证明，自己的风格才是最好的风格。

When the modern factors hit classical times, when elegant factors mix the strong factors, what kind of effect can produce? This space is just an illustration of how to look at and live the life: not following the massive, and not blindly cater to tide, adhere to its won unique taste, to pursue a rich culture, advocating elegant life.

The TV wall in the sitting room with four large silver fox marble Mosaic, thick, but a very simple sense, which make the sitting room full of traditional flavor. A group of black real leather sofa, sedate and luxury. The combination between hard pack arrangement of sofa and black mirror, plus modern science and technology which feeling metal sculpture, into the romantic color for the space, and match the main theme color in the restaurant. But the sitting room, kitchen room's aisles's three main views, and introduce the imported of quietly elegant coating show. Agile glass mirror to show the ark, under the black mirror reflection of light steel, display art show outstanding taste. In fact, it has been proven that own style is the best style.

STAR WARS
STAR WARS

STAR WARS
COLOMBO
Expo Express

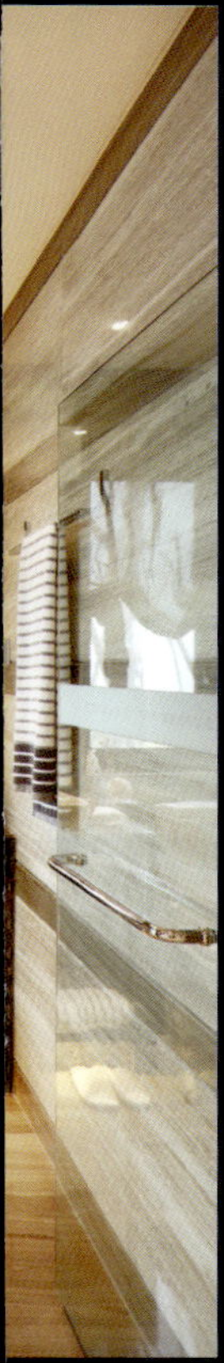

06

QINHUANGDAO BOYUESHAN BUILDING SALES OFFICE

秦皇岛铂悦山售楼处

Project name: Qinhuangdao Boyueshan Building Sales Office
Developer: Longji Taihe Real estate co.Ltd
Construction area: 2000 square meters
Using materials: Guizhou wood stone, black glass steel, senior wallpaper, leather, black and white roots, senior coatings, high solid real wood floor board, mirror stainless steel
Location of the project: Qinhuangdao city
Design time: In April, 2013

项目名称： 秦皇岛铂悦山售楼处
开发商： 隆基泰和实业有限公司
建筑面积： 2000 m^2
使用物料： 贵州木纹石材、黑镜钢、高级壁纸、皮革、黑白根、高级涂料、高级实木复合地板、镜面不锈钢
项目地点： 河北秦皇岛
设计时间： 2013年4月

PLATINUM YEARS
QINHUANGDAO
铂悦山

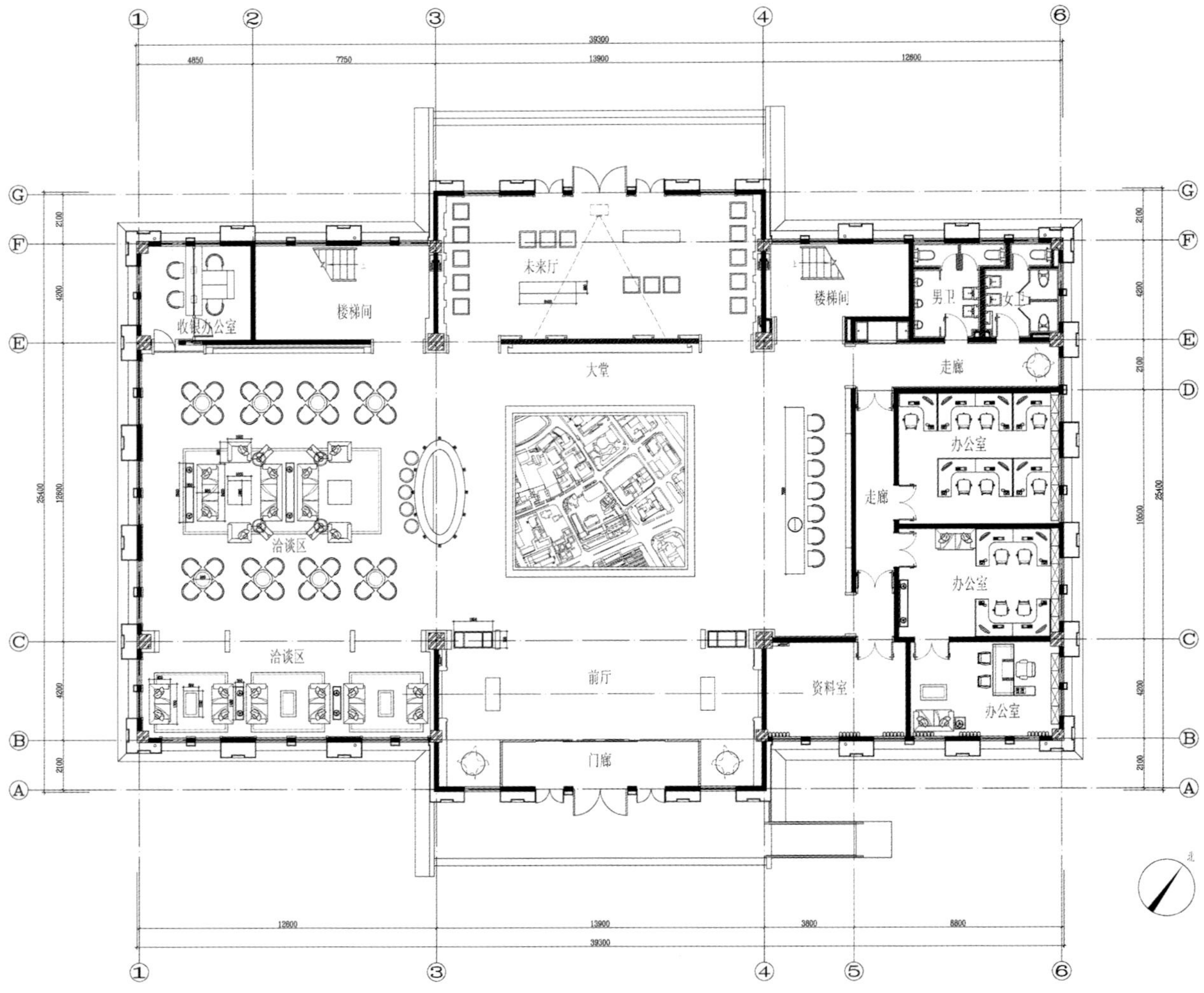

1F 平面

铂悦山项目以其鲜明的Art Deco（装饰艺术）建筑风尚闻名港城。本案的设计也承袭了这一风格。现代奢华融入少量的古典元素，再略带点中国风，使售楼处的整体格调得以升华。

本案在前台、接待大厅、洽谈区都使用了大量水晶，令整个场景倍感华丽。水吧上方的环形水晶串如同一帘纯净的瀑布，将售楼处整体较为庄严的感觉流露出一些浪漫色彩。大沙盘上方的大型水晶吊灯由设计师定制的水晶串吊挂而成，由周围射灯按照严格比例对其进行照射，有如众星捧月，璀璨夺目。

售楼处内部空间疏密有致，硬朗有型。大量的贵州木纹运用在地面、前台立面、门厅，黑镜钢不动声色地反射着室内的静物与活动的影像，理性中又显出至酷有型的一面。而陈列在黑镜钢展示架上的陶瓷艺术品，有的棱角分明、有的造型别致，让人难以忘怀。

从入口处映入眼帘的是气势恢弘的大面积石材，石材表面镶嵌着镜面不锈钢线条。刻意放大的空间尺度，简洁利落的线条，搭配洽谈区大气的条纹布艺沙发，都传递着设计师对现代奢华空间的演绎。硬朗的线条在整个空间延续，铺设遍布整个空间，营造接待中心一气呵成的空间延伸视觉效果，传递出项目摩登、理智、恒久的特质。

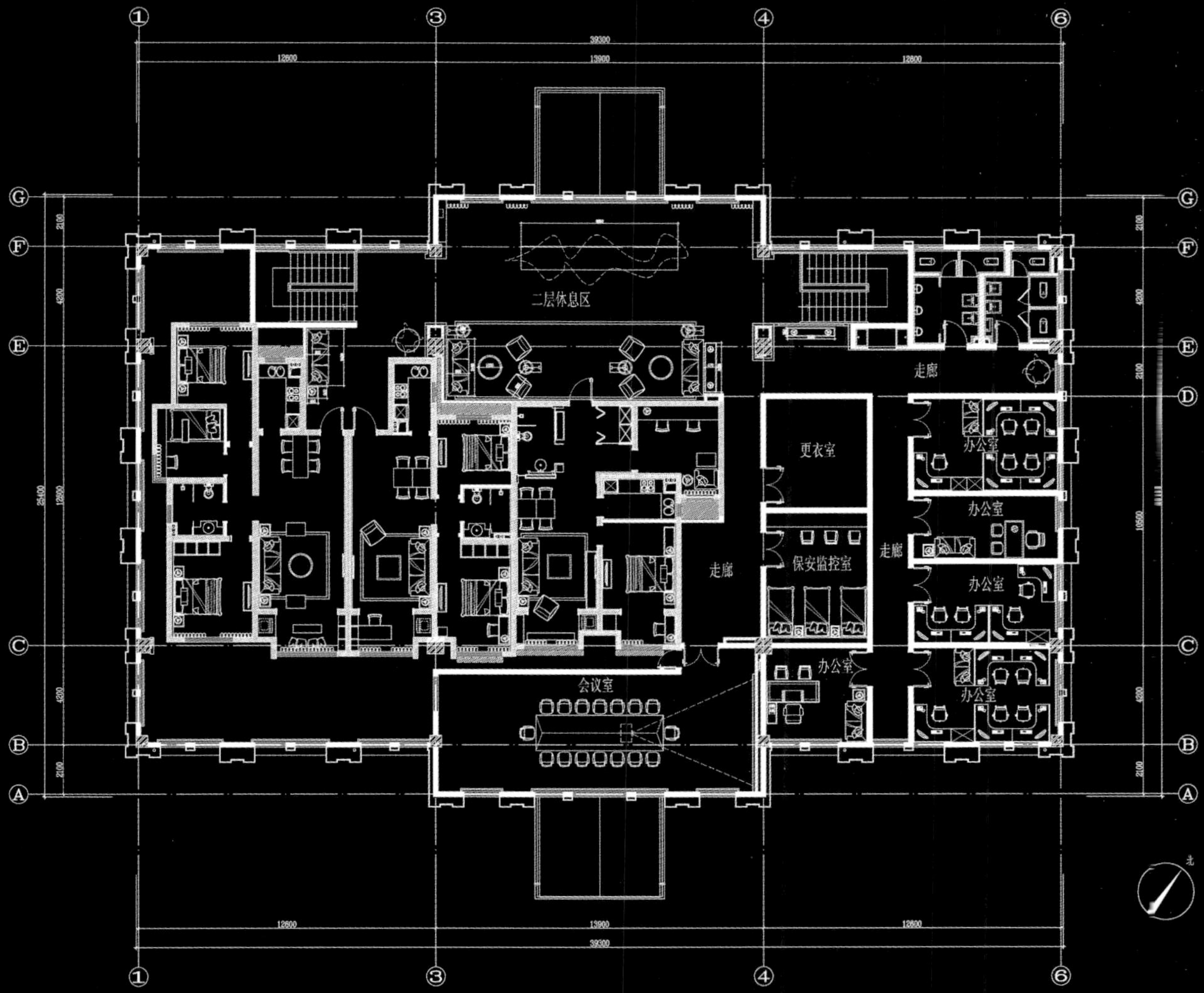

2F 平面

Boyue Mountain project project is known for its distinctive Art Deco building style of the country. The design of the case also took their cue from this style. Modern and luxury factors exist, but also contains a few classical factors, and plus some special Chinese fashion, which achieves the sublimation of the integral style of the sales office.

The case at the front desk, reception hall, discussion area, which all have used a large amount of crystal, make the whole scene feeling gorgeous. Water at the top of the ring crystal string like a curtain and pure waterfall, the sales department as a whole is relatively solemn feeling which reveals some romantic color. The big sand table includes the top of the large chandelier crystal by designer customized string hanging crystal, by around to shoot the light according to strict proportion to illuminate, as Zhongxingpengyue, Bright is dazzing.

The internal sales office has combined the space density, hale and hearty. Lot of Guizhou wood grain on the ground, front facade, hallway, black mirror steel quietly reflect the images from the interior of the still life and activities, rational but also cool type. And the displayed ceramic art or black mirror steel display rack, some angular, some chic modeling, to let people memorable.

From the entrance is grand large stone, the surface of stone materials is covered with mirror stainless steel lines. Deliberately magnified space scale, simple and agile line, to match the negotiation area atmospheric stripe cloth art sofa, convey the designer of modern luxury space of interpretation. Hale line continuation in whole space, laid across the space, build the same reception center space outspread vision effect, to deliver the qualities of modern, fashionable and reasonable factors and endurance.

YEARS
QINHUANGDAO
山

07

YUHE IMPRESSION THEME HOTEL

御河印象主题酒店

Project name: Yuhe Impression Theme Hotel
Developer: Datong Yuhe Impression Hospitality Management co.Ltd
Construction area: 12000 square meters
Using materials: new cream-colored stone materials, deep brown, Aegean grey, hard roll, senior silver foil wallpaper, leather, crystal, peirce white stone, grey wood, ebony facing senior, senior paint, senior carpet
Location of the project: Datong city, Shanxi Province
Design time: In July, 2012

项目名称： 御河印象主题酒店
客户： 大同御河印象酒店管理有限公司
建筑面积： 12000 m^2
使用物料： 新西米黄石材、深杭啡、爱琴海灰、硬包、高级银箔壁纸、皮革、水晶、雅士白石材、灰木纹、黑檀木饰面、高级涂料、高级地毯
项目地点： 山西 大同市
设计时间： 2012年7月

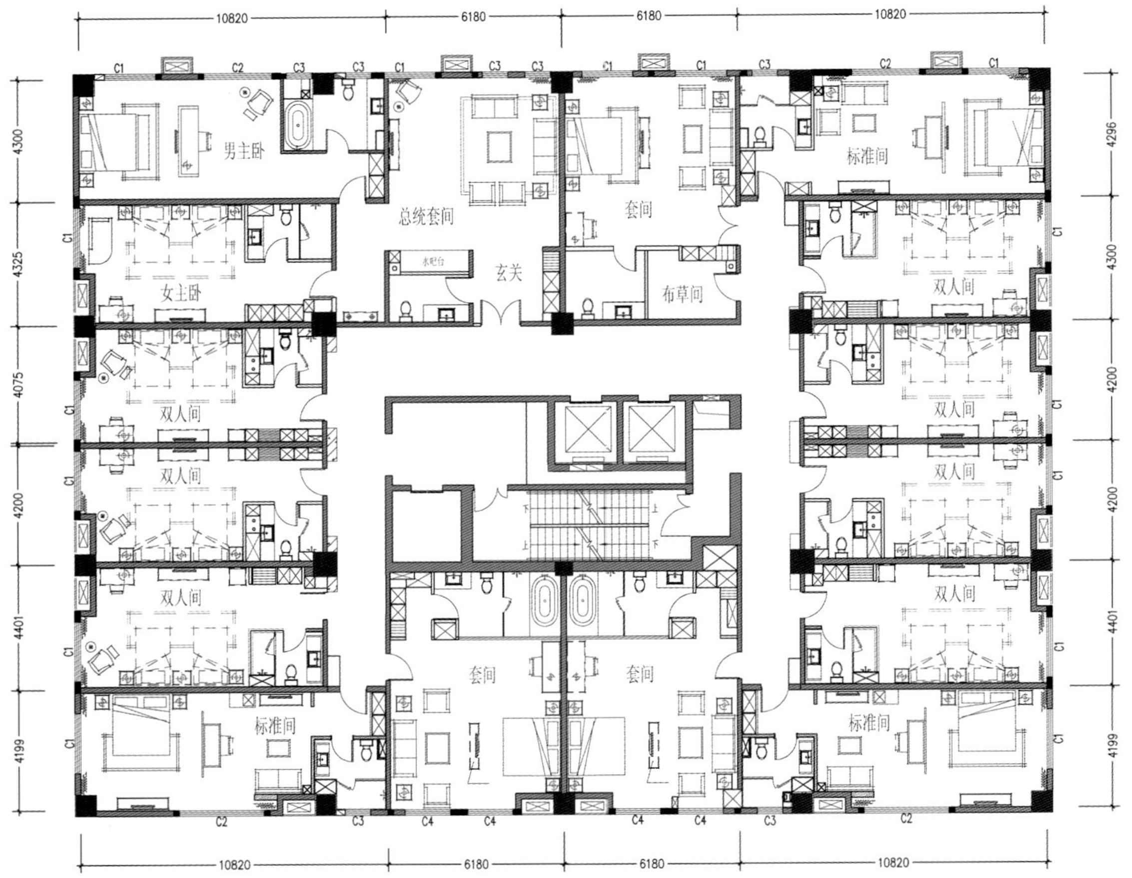

九层标层平面图

大同是一座文化古城。本案设计师将现代元素和传统文化结合在一起，以黑、白两种清雅颜色为主调，点缀以银灰、中国红，再融入水墨画、荷花灯、蒲扇等中式元素，给人一种中式古典的印象。

大厅入口采用大面积的窗格地拼，怀古气息扑面而来。前台背景墙的纹理采用中国古代宣纸的质感色彩拼贴而成。另一面背景墙则是设计师原创的一系列中国传统水墨画，旨在通过宁静高雅的禅意，为风尘仆仆的旅客洗去疲惫，栖息在纯美的艺术氛围中。

自助餐厅沿用了中国人传统的深色调。异形的石材前台，厚重、时尚，现代感与民族特色交融。前台背景墙采用木饰面、黑钢条，结合素雅的壁纸营造出舒适的光感和立体感。存储食物的餐台上方，有一排柱状的古铜色灯具，别具匠心。

用餐休息区地面一致采用深色的木纹砖。橙红色的皮质沙发在整个场景中起到了冷暖对比的作用，温馨典雅，不显一丝压抑。以大雁为灵感的水晶灯，光影交叠，绚丽多姿。纵观全景，就像一幅清新素雅的中国古典画卷。

Datong is a cultural ancient city. This case stylist combines modern elements and traditional culture together, give priority to tone with black and white colors, the ornament with silver grey, red China, put the ink, wash, the latterns of ancient Chinese into it, which give a sense of classical Chinese.

The entrance Hall adopts the pane to spell of large area, meditate on the breath. The texture of the front desk setting wall is in Chinese ancient rice paper piecing up the simple sense of color. Setting wall on the other side is the original idea of the designer of the traditional Chinese ink painting, through quiet elegant Zen, to relax exhausted, travel-stained passengers perched on a pure artistic atmosphere.

The traditional Buffet restaurants has used the Chinese ancient style. The stone material of the different character at the front desk, thick, fashion, modern factor and national characteristics.The front desk adopt background wall with wood veneer, black steel,combined with the simple but elegant wallpaper, which creates a comfortable sense of light and stereo feeling. At the front of the counter for Storing food, a row of cylindrical bronze lamps and lanterns, with unique sense of craftsmanship.

Dining area is covered with dark wood grain brick. Orange red leather sofa in the whole scene, warm and elegant, do not show a little depressed. The crystalline light of geese as inspiration, light and shadow overlap, colorful. Throughout a panoramic view, it is like a pure and fresh, simple but elegant classical Chinese ancient picture.

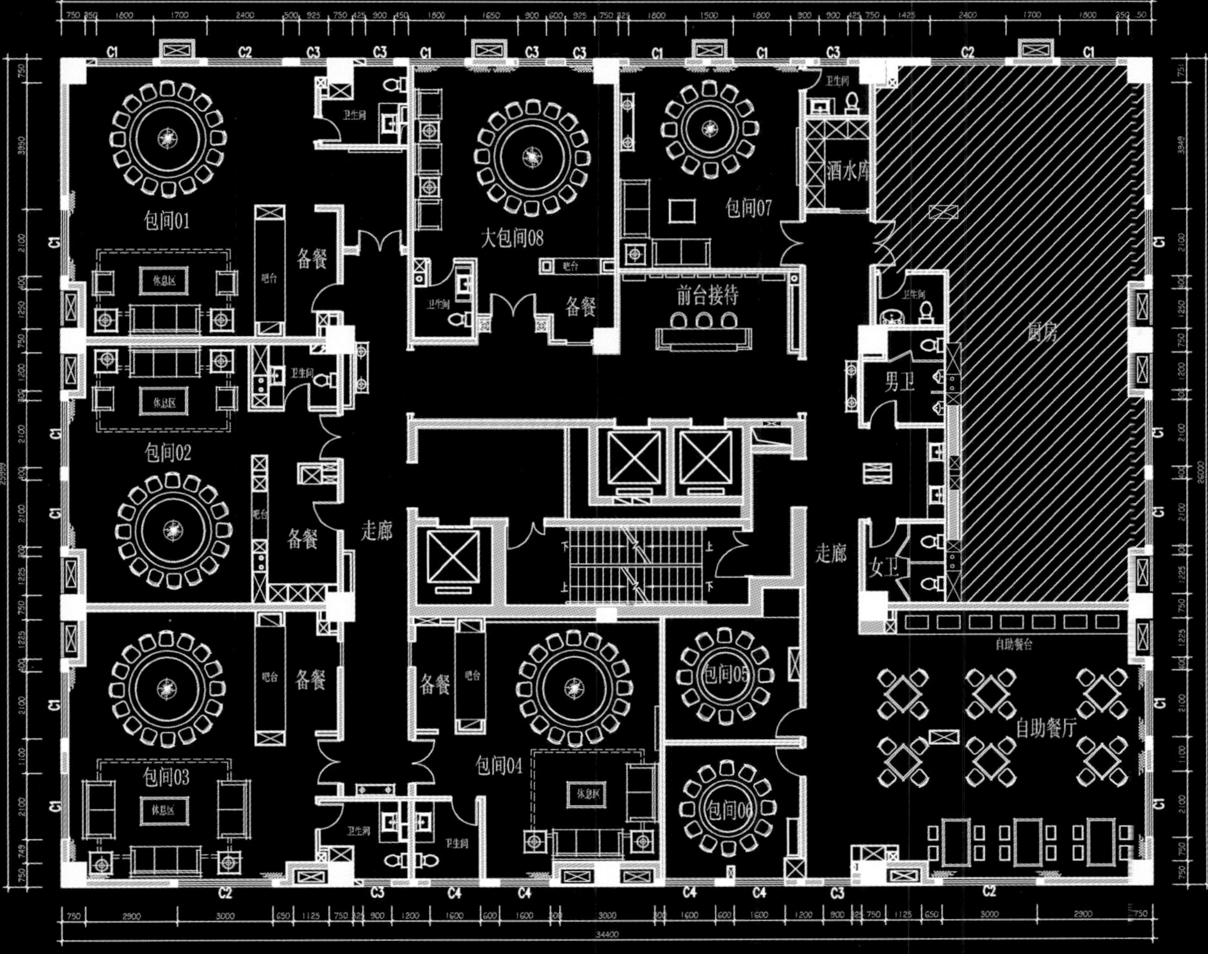

顶层十四层餐饮平面图

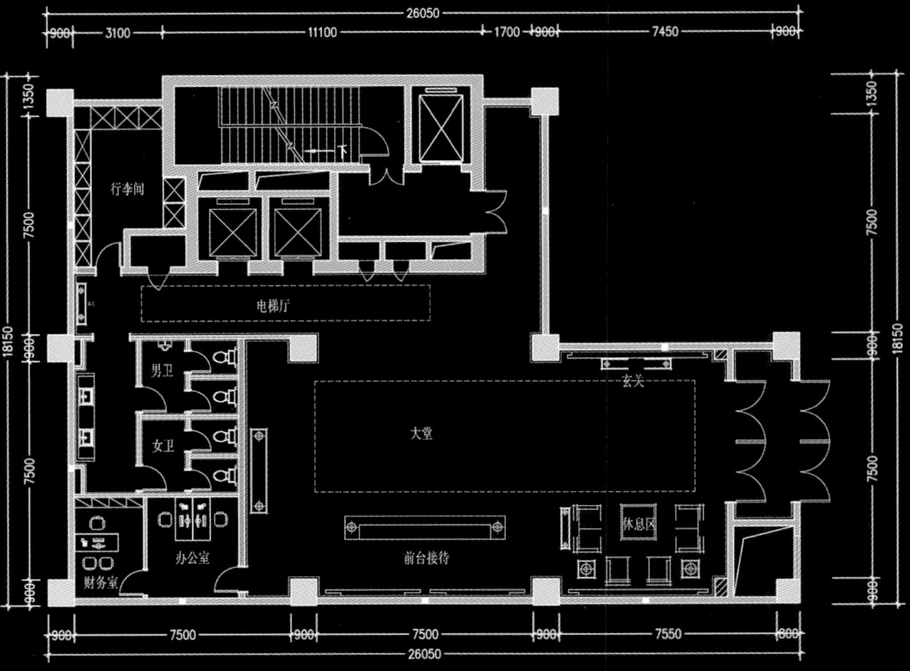

首层平面图

08

BEIJING GUANSHANYUE A MOUNTAIN VILLA MODEL HOUSE

北京观山悦A别墅样板房

Project name: Beijing Guanshanyue A Mountain Villa Model House
Developer: Beijing Science Park Construction (Group) co.Ltd
Construction Area: 620 square meters
Using materials: Moonlight cream-colored stone, teak veneer, senior wallpaper, leather, high quality hard package, advanced coatings, silver foil, advanced solid real wood floor board
Project location: Beijing
Design time: In March, 2012

项目名称： 北京观山悦A别墅样板房
开发商： 北京科技园建设(集团)股份有限公司
建筑面积： 620 m^2
使用物料： 月光米黄石材、柚木饰面、高级壁纸、皮革、优质硬包、高级涂料、银箔、高级实木复合地板
项目地点： 北京
设计时间： 2012年3月

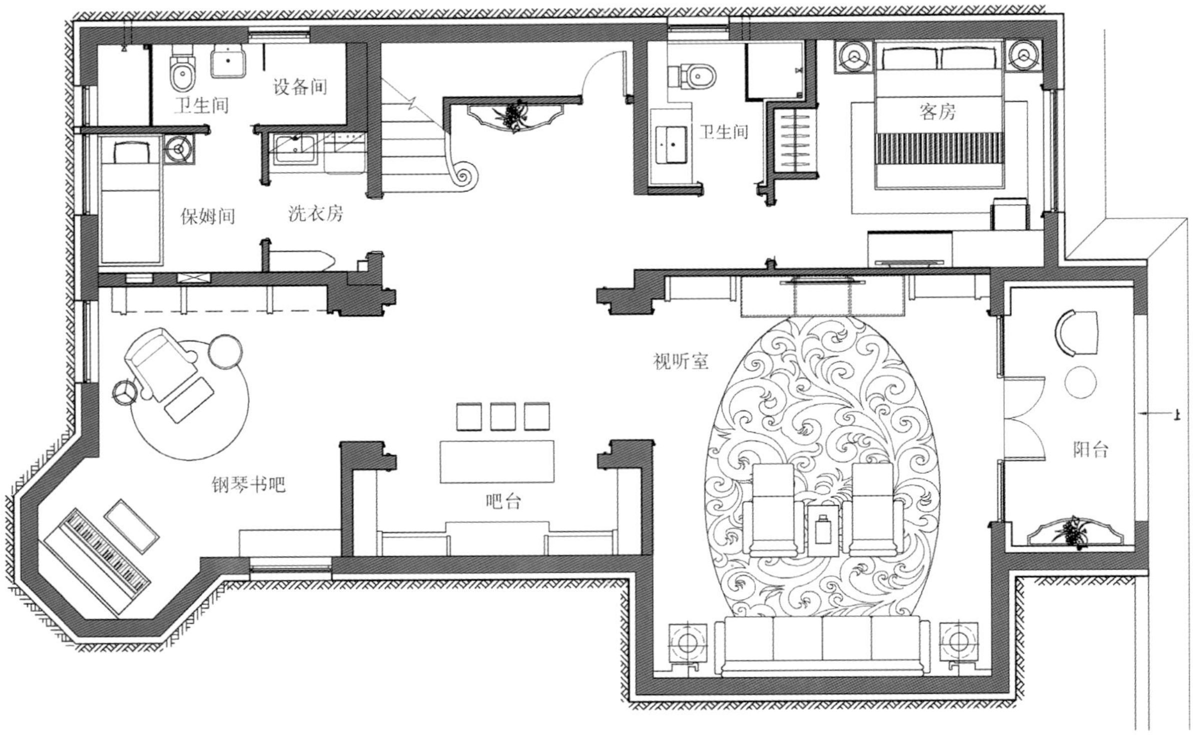

负一层平面

回归田园、亲近山水，这大概是每个城市人的向往。考虑到本案项目依山而筑，周围有优美的山水景观，设计师通过一系列极富美式风情的装饰元素，倾力打造了一个舒适浪漫、悠然自得的乡情空间。

门、窗大量运用了拱式设计，营造出田园生活般的舒适与宁静。客厅家具线条干练，体积粗狂，掩不住的美式奢华。大花瓣窗帘，碎花朵地毯，清婉美丽。肌理丰富的木饰面，镶嵌着自然的浅色花壁，木的质朴与花的温柔水乳交融。顶部的金箔壁纸在水晶吊灯的照耀下，犹如繁星闪烁。家里的每一个角落，无不舒适惬意，悠然自得。

水吧区的地板颜色就像浪漫的葡萄酒，在灯光的烘托下，散发着迷人的气息，这就是谁也离不开的，温暖的，家。

Return to the rural park, close to the landscape, this is probably the pursuit of every citizen of the city. Considering the project is built around the mountain, and also surrounded by beautiful mountains and waters landscape, the designer use a series of adornment full of extremely rich feelings, take every effort to create a comfortable and romantic carefree and leisurely rural space.

The door and the window use the arch design in great quantities, to build a comfortable and quiet environment like the rural life. The sitting room furniture line has rapid volume, hide the American luxury. Big petals curtain, carpet of flowers, beauty writers. Rich texture of wood veneer, studded with natural light color with flower wall, the gentle quality of the flower is put into it. On the top of the gold foil wallpaper in the crystal droplight, the stars are twinkling. Every corner of the family, the people will feel comfortable and relaxed.

The floor color of the water area is like the romantic wine, under the lights of the foil, the water area sends out the charming atmosphere. Because this belongs to everyone warm home.

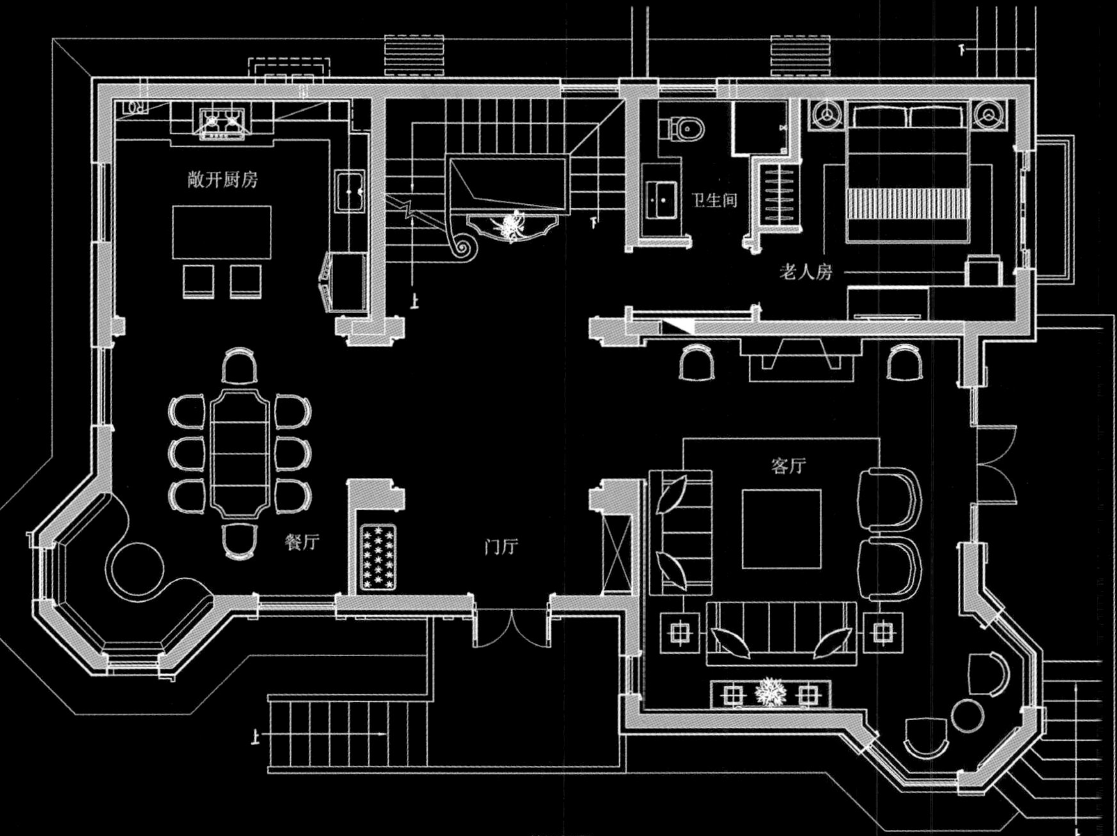

首层平面

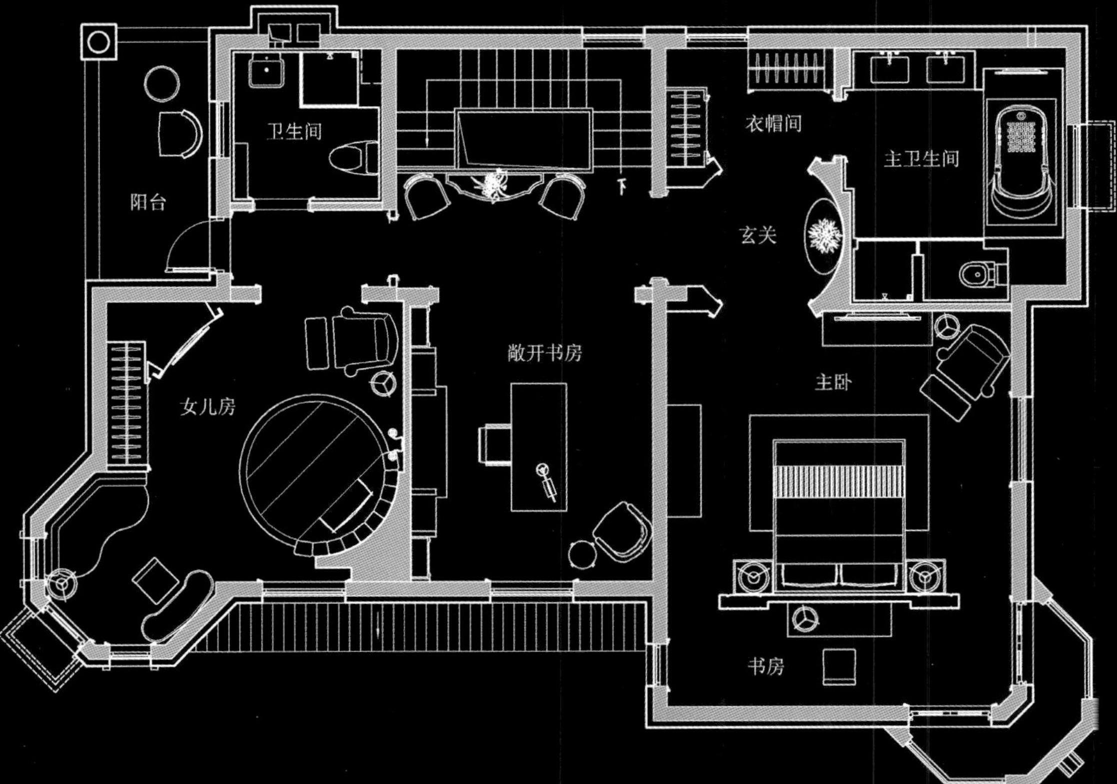

二层平面

09

QINHUANGDAO RUNDIQINGYUN NEW CHINESE MODEL HOUSE

秦皇岛润地青云新中式样板房

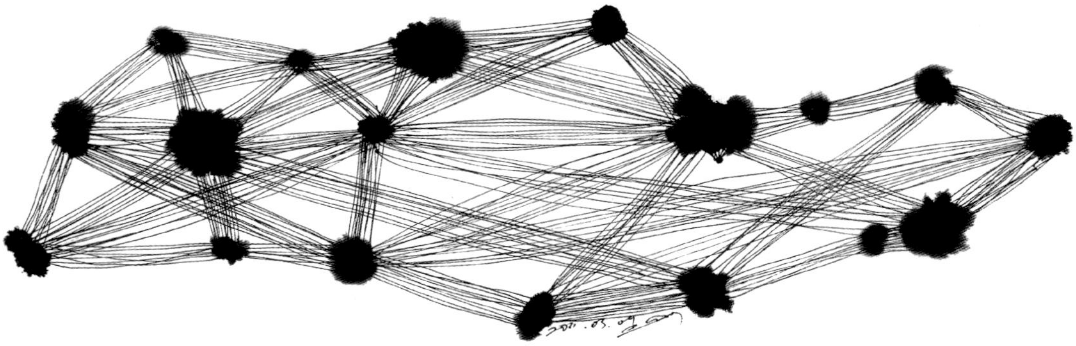

Project name: Qinhuangdao Rundiqingyun New Chinese Model House
Developer: Rundi Real Estate
Construction Area: 120 square meters
Using materials: Silver mirror, ash wood, computer carve patterns, designs on woodwork, ebony facing materials, senior paint, senior carpet
Project location: Qinhuangdao
Design time: In April, 2011

项目名称： 秦皇岛润地青云新中式样板房
开发商： 润地地产
建筑面积： 120 m^2
使用物料： 银镜、灰木纹、电脑雕刻雕花、黑檀木饰面、高级涂料、高级地毯
项目地点： 河北秦皇岛
设计时间： 2011年4月

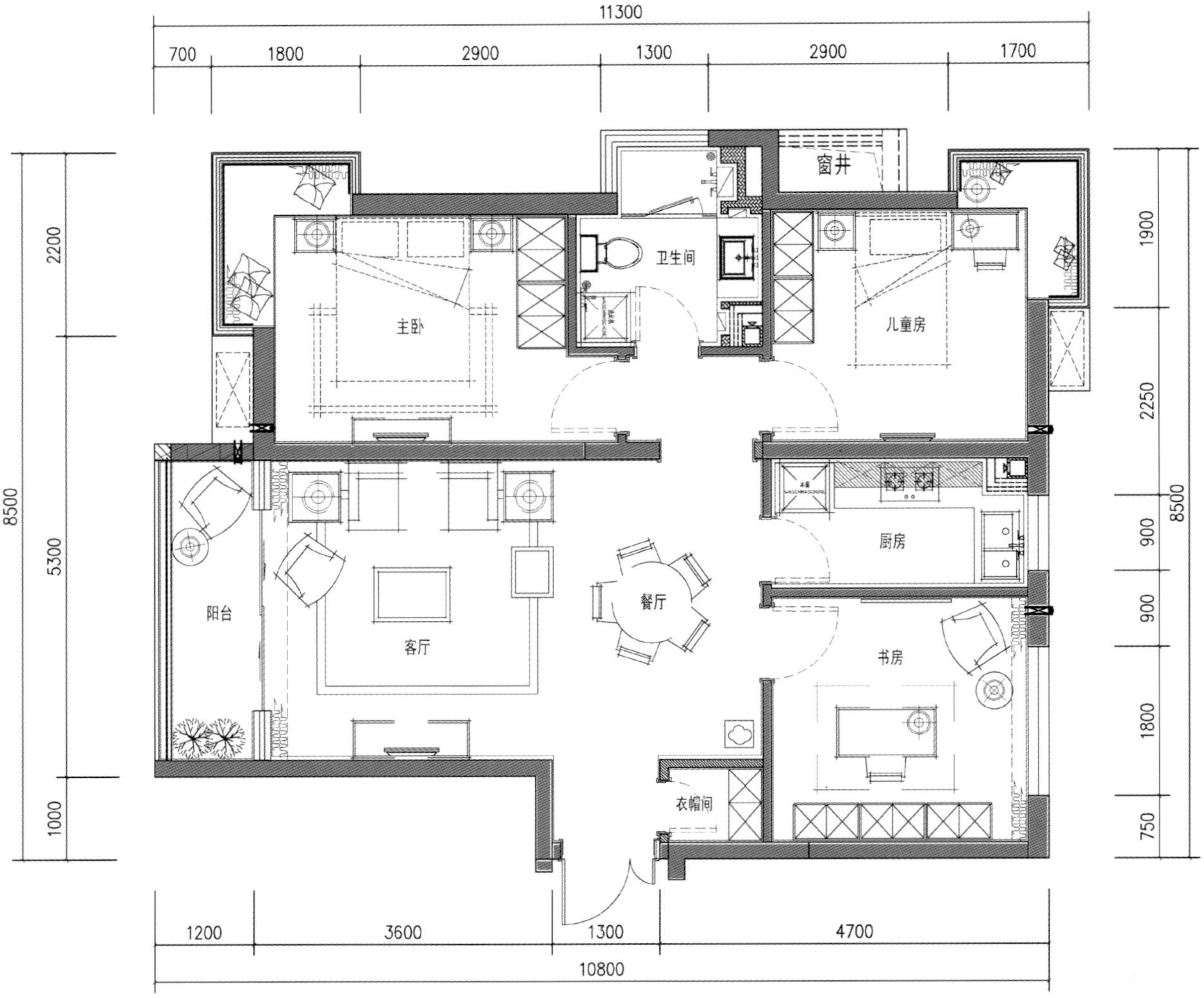

平面布置图

本案的设计可谓将装饰材料运用到极致。大量的深色木质线条，交错而又延伸地贯穿于各个空间，勾勒出新中式的硬朗外表。床头背景墙仅仅由亚麻壁纸和木线条框组成，自然简约，效果出彩。深色古木的做旧家具上是不动声色的奢华，梳妆台的边缘镶嵌着金色烤漆花纹。在光和材质的相互作用下，整个居室空间爽朗大气，再加上东方的沉静韵味，尽显优雅与庄重的双重品质。

主卧顶棚的铁艺中式吊灯，小巧精致，让空间的古意气质得到升华，同时又和墙上的饰品形成呼应，亮点相互交错。各种现代感与历史感完美结合的软装饰，营造了浓郁的文化气息和温暖的家居。

The design of the case is to use the adornment materials to the extreme extent. Large amounts of dark wood line, crossing and also extends throughout the space, appearance of new Chinese style with hale and hearty. The head of the bed is composed of flax wallpaper and wooden line box, natural simplicity effect. Dark ancient wood is costly, and the dressing desk is painted with golden painting decorative pattern. Under the interaction of light and material, the whole bedroom is full of space and bright atmosphere, coupled with quiet charm of the east, all show elegant and grave quality.

The light on the master bedroom with iron chandelier style, exquisite, put the situation to distillation, which let the space temperament improve in the ancient times, and to match the decoration on the wall at the same time, highlights the mutual crisscross. All kinds of soft adornment of perfect combination of modern sense and historical sense, to create a rich culture and a warm home.

10

BAODING CITY FUTURE CAPITAL SALES OFFICE

保定未来城售楼处

Project name: Baoding city Future Capital Sales Office
Developers: Longji taihe industrial co., LTD
Construction area: 1200 square meters
Using materials: copper, new west cream-colored, Aegean grey, silver mirror, black mirror, senior wallpaper, tawny glasses, black and white roots, advanced solid wood floor
Project location: Baoding
Design time: in March 2013

项目名称： 保定未来城售楼处
开发商： 隆基泰和实业有限公司
建筑面积： 1200 m^2
使用物料： 铜板、新西米黄、爱琴海灰、银镜、黑镜、高级壁纸、茶镜、黑白根、高级实木地板
项目地点： 河北保定
设计时间： 2013年3月

FANTASY
LAND
未来城

前台接待大厅入口处金属镂空雕花的延伸线条，镶嵌在玻璃围幕中，除了保证良好透光性外，也赋予量体轻盈感。

室内空间元素呼应建筑外部调性，用黑白灰以及米黄来演绎低调奢华的性格。前台接待厅的地拼运用不同色彩的石材，其相互之间的比例通过严谨精算，用最简单明确的语言，演绎出迎宾大厅不显而张的沉稳气势。

沙盘及洽谈区域的车边茶镜吊顶，安装的是巨型水晶组合吊灯。顶部多层叠级，水流般的直线倾泻而下，光影如梭，给人以高速公路般强烈的速度感。大量的水晶在光的作用下，唤醒了人们对新时代的未来感，引领宾客步入这“未来城”住宅公区的探索之旅。

纵观场景空间，设计师采用象征奢华的水晶灯、银箔、层次感十足的射灯，意图延伸访客的视觉感受，在售楼处当中就能体现未来现代感的家居空间，舒适、时尚、无可挑剔。整个场景在材料的选择上采用高雅的色彩搭配，亮面的浅色茶镜和各种色彩的石材以及大量雍容华丽的丝质布料，创造出一个时尚、华丽而又丰富的售楼处。

In the front desk reception hall, at the entrance to the extension of carve patterns or designs on woodwork metal lines, embedded in the glass side curtain, apart from ensuring good light transmission, and also give a sense of quantity body with light feeling.

Interior space element echo the external building tonality, with black and white ash cream-colored to deduce a low-key costly character. Front desk reception hall is used by different color of stone materials, the proportion of each other is through strict actuarial science, in the most simple and clear language, deduce doesn't welcome hall in a steady momentum.

Sand table and discussion area , which is installed with a giant crystal droplight combinations. More than the top layer. The flow of linear pour down, light and shadow passed by quickly, which give a person with the highway, strong sense of speed. A large amount of crystal is under the function of the light, awaken the people to the future of the new era, lead the guests to enter the housing and the city of the future exploration.

Throughout the scene space, the designer adopt the symbol fo the luxury crystal lamp, silver foil, the lights have administrative levels of feelings, in order to extend the visual feelings of visitors, in the sales office, you can experience the furniture space of the future modernism, comfortable, fashionable and impeccable. The whole scene on the choice of material, based on the collocation of the elegant, bright light yellow coloured glass and all kinds of colors of the stone, and a large number of natural and graceful luxuriant silk fabrics, to create a fashionable, gorgeous and rich sales office.

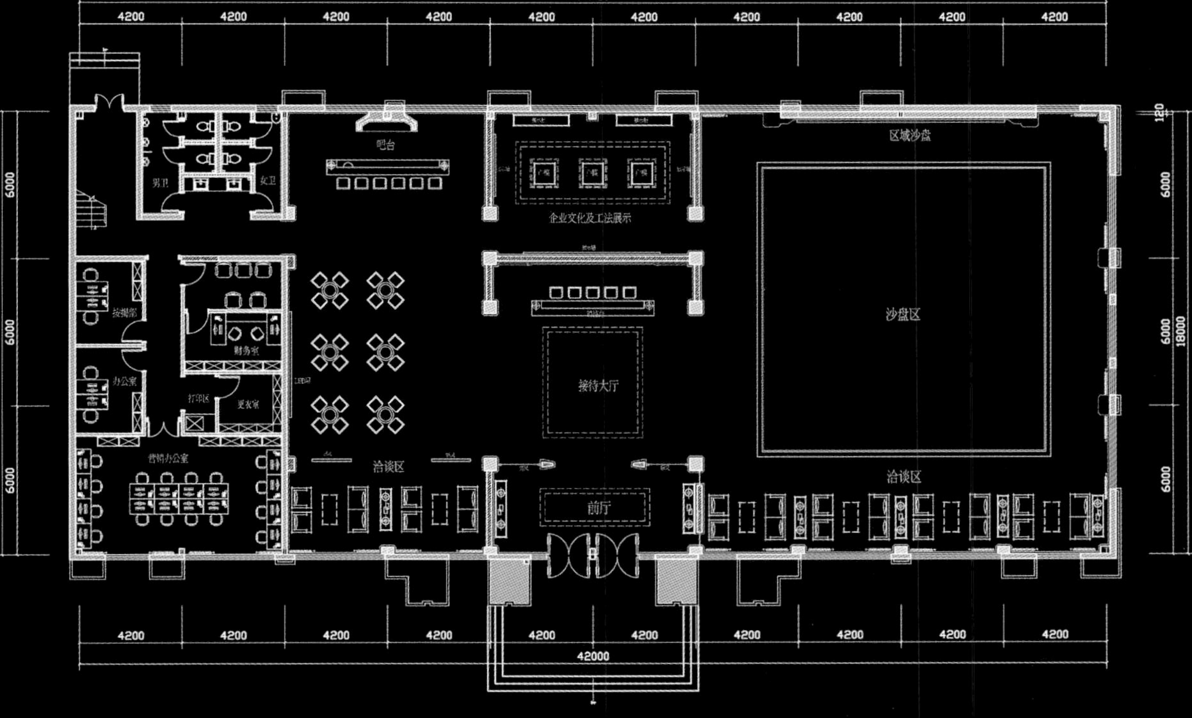

首层平面布置

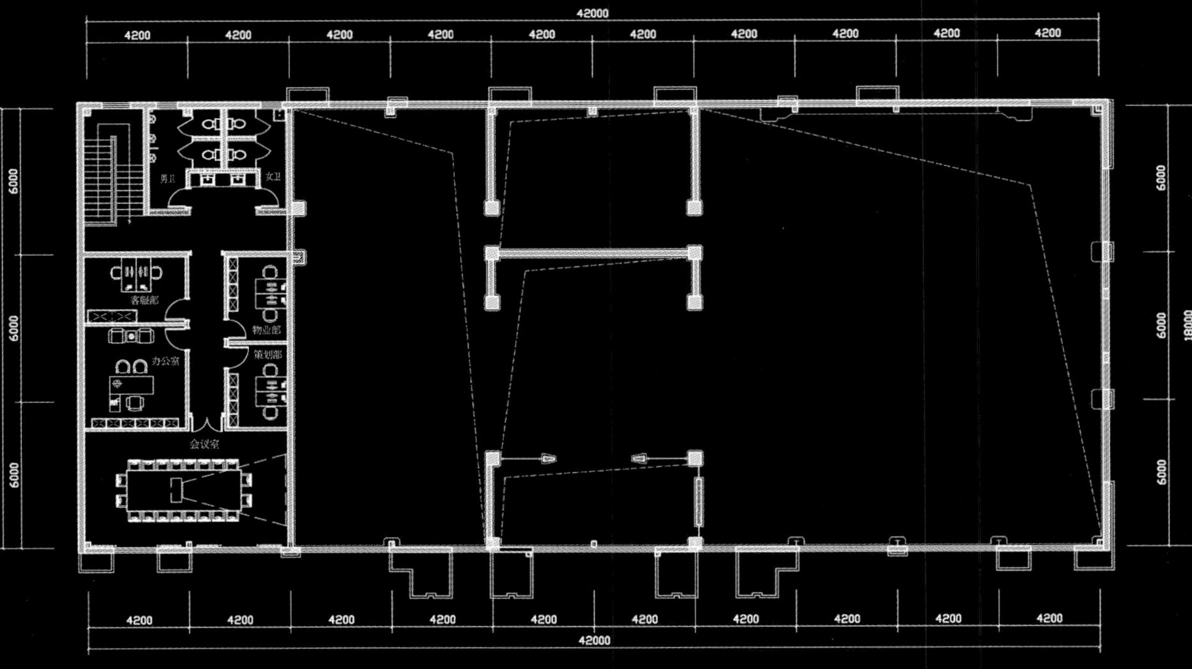

二层平面布置

接待热线:

BEIJING XIANGJIANG CONTEMPORARY AND CONTRACTED GARDEN VILLA MODEL HOUSE

北京香江花园现代简约别墅精装修样板房

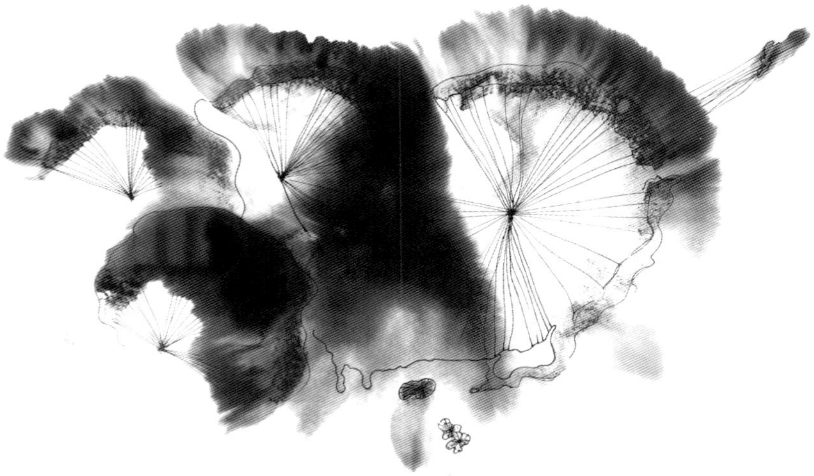

Project name: Beijing Xiangjiang Contemporary and Contracted Garden Villa Model House
Developers: HongKong land holdings co., Ltd
Construction area: 500 square meters
Using material: black steel, wood veneer, new west cream-colored stone, senior wallpaper, leather, senior paintings, high solid real wood floor board, silver mirror
Project location: Beijing
Design time: in April 2012

项目名称：北京香江花园现代简约别墅精装修样板房
开发商：香港置地控股有限公司
建筑面积：500 m^2
使用物料：黑钢、木饰面、新西米黄石材、高级壁纸、皮革、高级涂料、高级实木复合地板、银镜
项目地点：北京
设计时间：2012年4月

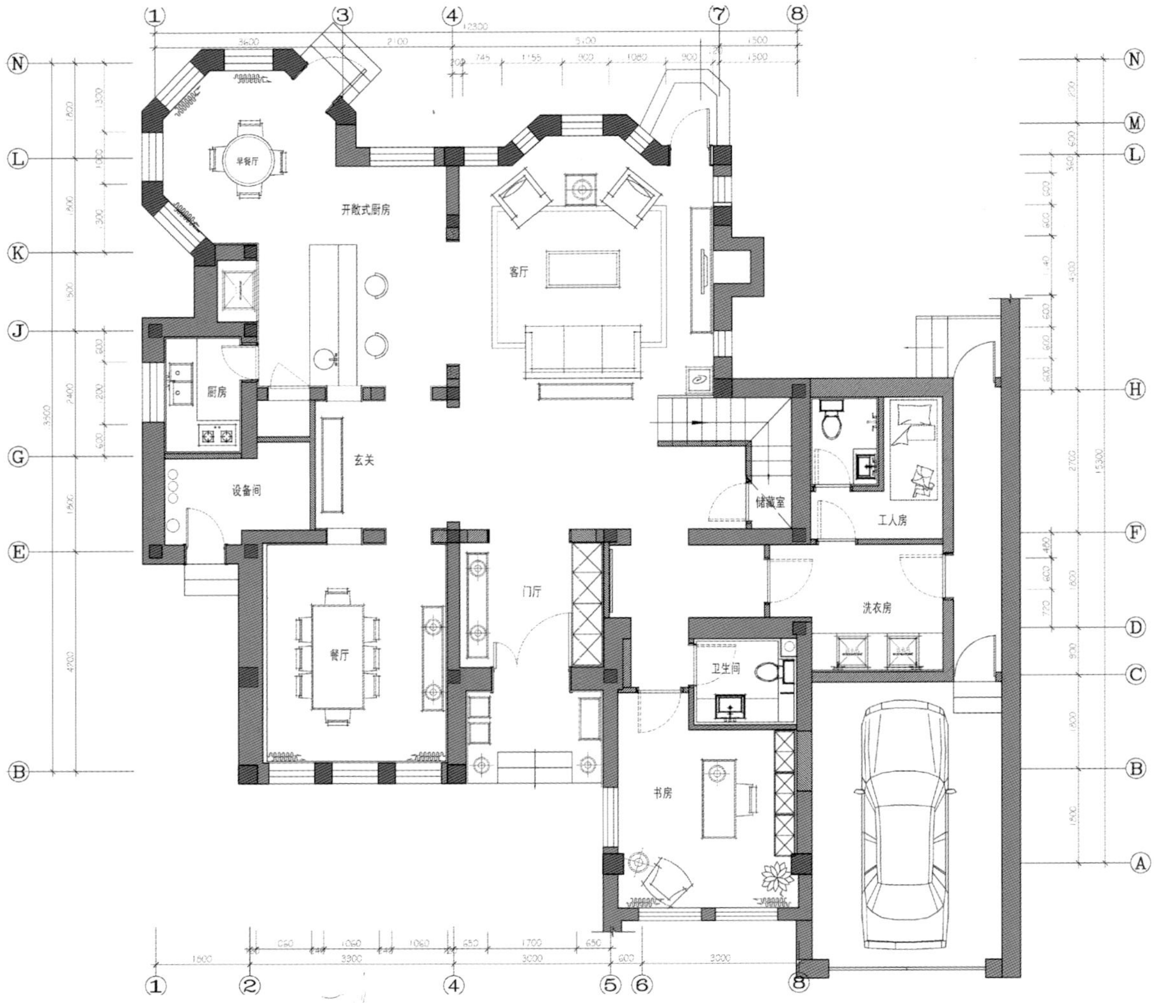

首层平面布置图

本案软装设计以现代都市风格为主。现代人的生活快节奏、高频率、满负荷。人们在这日趋繁忙的生活中，渴望能够得到一种彻底放松、调节精神的空间。“以减至简、简而纯美”是本案的设计重点。

阳光从窗户斜斜地照进来，映在了茶几上的书角，温暖柔和的气息荡漾在每一处角落。整体色系以咖啡色为主体，大面积的咖啡色不仅能营造出室内的温馨氛围，而且还能烘托出极强的品质感，并融合贯穿成一个整体的优雅色调，通过材质变化达到视觉上的冲击。局部用一些绿色和白色作为前两者的补充与调和，空间更显灵动。

本案在材质上，大面积使用木饰面和石材，线条简约流畅；又大量使用钢化玻璃、不锈钢等新型材料作为辅材，给人带来新潮时尚、不受拘束的感觉。彩色靠垫、餐桌布的陪衬，显示出色彩对比的美感，又流露出简约舒适的居住情怀。

The soft outfit design is given priority to modern urban style in the case. The high rhythm of modern people, high frequency and full load, people have to accept the point of total relaxing, mediating the spirit space. "Pure beauty" in to Jane, and Jane is the design key of the case.

The sunshine shed from the windows, reflected in the angle of the books on the table, warm breath of soft ripples in every corner. The major body of overall color is coffee color, which creates a indoor warm atmosphere, but also can foil a strong sense of quality, throughout and combined into a whole elegant sense, by the impact of the material change to achieve the vision shock. Part of it is used from both green and white materials, harmonic and inspirational space.

From the perspective of the materials on the case, a large square meter is widely used by the wood veneer and stone materials, contracted and fluent line; And extensively use of tempered glass, stainless steel and other new materials as auxiliary materials, which give a person the feeling of trendy fashion, uninhibited. The foil color cushion, table cloth, which show the aesthetic feeling of color contract, and also reveals the simple and comfortable living feelings.

二层平面布置图

Sewing
New Complete Guide to Sewing

12

BEIJING GUANSHANYUE SALES OFFICE

北京观山悦售楼处

Project name: Beijing Guanshanyue Sales Office
Developers: Beijing Science Park Construction (Group) co., Ltd
Construction area: 1000 square meters
Using materials: cherry wood veneer, cream-colored stone, pits wallpaper, high quality hard box, deep brown, senior paintings, silver foil, advanced solid wood floor
Project location: Beijing
Design time: in March 2012

项目名称： 北京观山悦售楼处
开发商： 北京科技园建设(集团)股份有限公司
建筑面积： 1000 m^2
使用物料： 樱桃木饰面、米黄石材、麻面壁纸、优质硬包、深杭啡、高级涂料、银箔、高级实木地板
项目地点： 北京
设计时间： 2012年3月

領秀
大中关村 城市山水独栋

本案空间以深咖色为主色调。通过多处不同材质、不同色彩的对比，使整个空间动静结合、张弛有度，营造出轻松优雅的销售氛围。前台背景墙主要采用不同深浅的木板，层层递进，有序拼合，呈现出一种轻松的律动。设计师充分结合光和材料原有的属性，在背景墙四周加上暖色灯带，将天然木材的质感完美表现。奢华的水晶吊灯下，不规则形的接待台将方方正正的横梁、背景墙、大沙盘逐个打破，赋予整个空间和谐又不失活力的味道。小巧精致的壁灯、生机勃勃的绿植，在设计师的精心搭配下，展颜欢待每一位身临其中的访客。偌大的接待厅，初入时只觉气势如虹，走进了，却有家庭会客厅般的温馨感受。

洽谈区是厚重的欧式新古典，既考虑到私密性，又处处体现了非凡的格调。极具品质感的皮质沙发，清新自然的花艺点缀其间。深色与浅色的沙发间隔陈列，一放一收，既有视觉的冲击力，又大气庄重。

卫生间采用不同材质将不规则的面进行合理的分割，粗犷的深杭啡地面纹理和细腻的木饰面墙面产生对比又能完美的融合在一起。造型独特的台盆，点亮了整个空间，使得空间不沉闷，有活力。

水吧区设计了强大的储物空间。与面积不大的水吧对比，丝毫不显突兀。大气利落的铜质壁灯相应左右，别致贵气的三盏小吊灯尽显欧式古典小镇的浪漫情怀。

纵观整个售楼处的设计，优雅、厚重、充满质感。设计师一丝不苟的专业精神，注入了每一处雕花，每一个抱枕，甚至是壁纸花纹的深浅之中。

The deep coffee color is the primary color in the space of this case. Through the comparisons of several different materials and different colors, which make the overall space full of dynamic and static state, to create a relaxed and elegant sales environment. Front desk setting wall mainly adopts different shades of wood, progressive transformation, orderly split, to present a kind of relaxed rhythm. Designers combine the light and the original material properties, around the background walls with warm light, will be natural wood texture and perfect performance. Under the luxurious crystal light, irregular reception will square beams, setting wall, large sand break them one by one, leading to the taste of whole space with harmony and vitality. Cabinet and delicate wall lamp, vibrant green plant, under the designer's elaborate collocation, to welcome every visitor in the situation. In the reception hall, you will fee majestic when you once enter, and when you arrive there, but a different experience will occur to you, the warm feeling like family saloon.

The discussion area is thick neo-classical European, both considering the privacy factor, the space embodies the special style. The quality leather sofa has extreme quality, pure and fresh floral ornament is put into it, dark color and light color has interval display, a close one, both have visual shock and solemn atmosphere.

Toilet uses different materials to divide the irregular surfaces, rough deep brown ground texture and fine wood veneer, which contrasts and blend together. Unique in the basin, lit up the whole space, which make the space energetic.

Water area designs powerful storage space. Compared with small water, do not show abrupt. Atmospheric agile copper wall lamp exists, corresponding to the left and right sides, chic and three expensive small lights, which shows the romantic feelings of the European ancient town.

Throughout the entire floor design, elegant, massiness, full of simple sense. The meticulous professionalism of the designer, which is injected with each place of carve patterns or designs on woodwork, each hold pillow, and even the depth of the decorative pattern of the wallpaper.

机房
收纳空间
男卫
洗手台
女卫
水吧区
保安室
视听室
过厅
洽谈区
沙盘区
户模
销控台

首层平面图

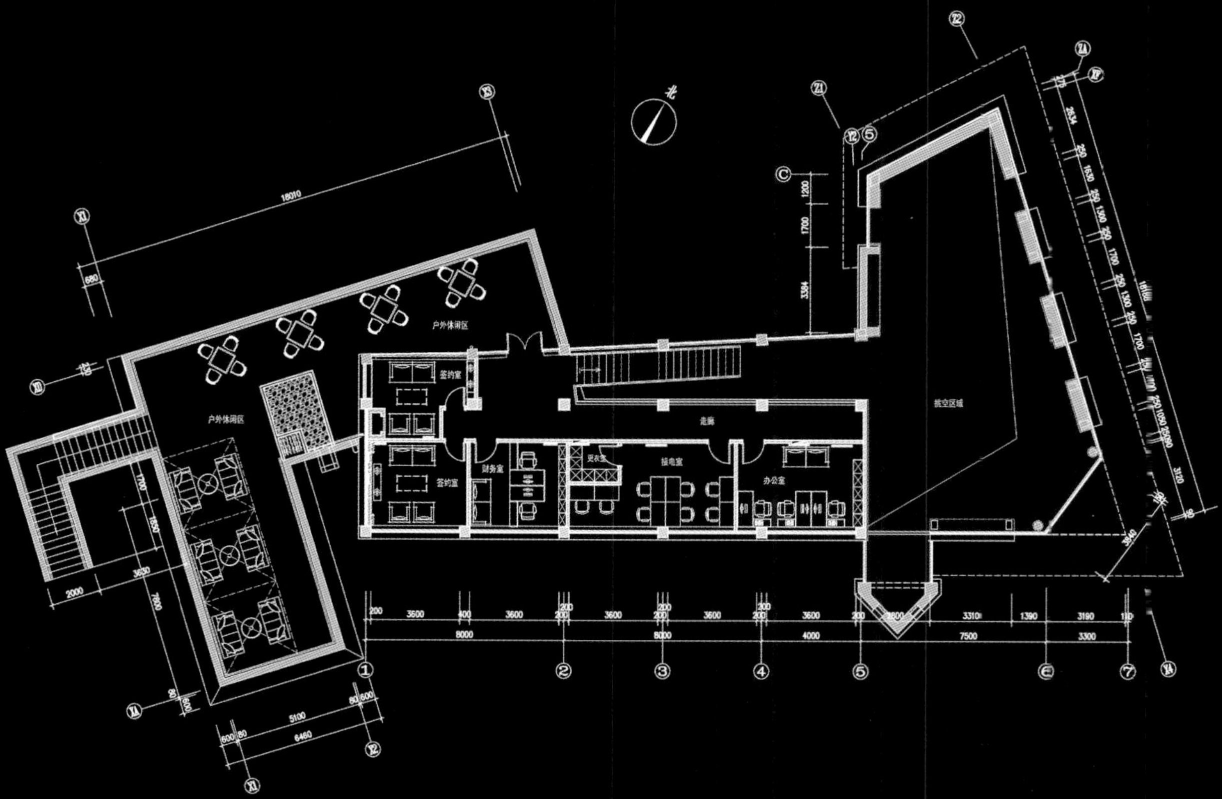
户外休闲区
签约室
财务室
更衣室
接电室
办公室
走廊
挑空区域

二层平面图

領秀
觀山悦

13

QINHUANGDAO RUNDIQINGYUN HONG KONG STYLE EXAMPLE ROOM

秦皇岛润地青云港式样板间

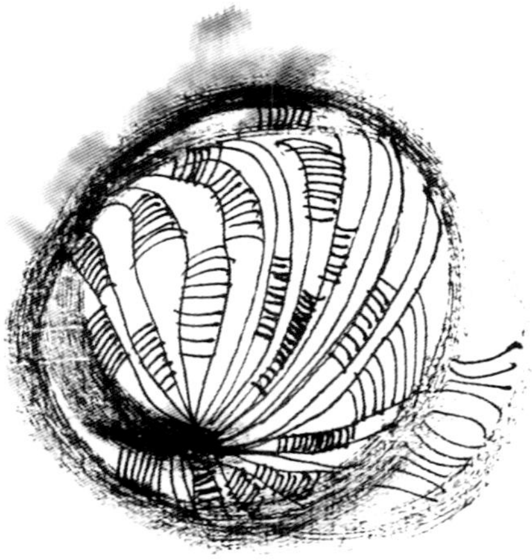

Project name: Qinhuangdao Rundiqingyun Hong Kong style Example Room
Developers: Rundi real estate co., Ltd
Construction area: 120 square meters;
Using material: silver mirror, ash wood, Anna cream-colored, black mirror, ebony stone facing senior, senior paint, carpet;
Location of project: Qinhuangdao
Design time: in March 2011

项目名称： 秦皇岛润地青云港式样板间
客户： 润地房产有限公司
建筑面积： 80 m^2
使用物料： 银镜、灰木纹、莎安娜米黄石材、黑镜、黑檀木饰面、高级涂料、高级地毯
项目地点： 河北秦皇岛
设计时间： 2012年3月
完工时间： 2012年6月软装工程／艺术品

创造独具个性的空间环境是每个室内设计师的共同追求，但个性不是将材料、家具、织物等元素简单叠加和堆砌就能达到的，如果摒弃了对建筑内在结构、体块和空间内涵这些隐性因素的认识和感知，个性就成了无根之木、无源之水。

在本案的设计中，设计者更注重空间共性的表达，从尊重建筑内在精神入手，运用具有一致性和规律性的表达手法来处理空间的体块关系、收口关系、光影关系，利用纵向的立面设计，大块面的墙面铺装和简洁的家具陈设，挖掘建筑自身的魅力，还原居住空间——“家”的本真概念。同时，设计师又根据空间自身的背景和场所感，通过对比、协调、统一等设计手法进行二次创作，通过家具风格的定位，配饰的选择和装饰材料的质感这些显性的元素来塑造属于这一空间的独特气质。

例如餐厅墙面整块的拼装银镜装饰，客厅背景墙以及休息区中略带东南亚元素的墙饰，这些简练纯粹的直线条的家具与大体块的空间布局在纵向和横向上相互穿插，构架风格统一的硬质空间。而客厅内朴素典雅的织物和现代家具渗透出的清爽品质感，色彩上素色调的强烈对比又迎合了空间宁静、简素的人文家居风格。这些设计元素密不可分，与空间浑然一体，使空间装饰和设计具有了唯一性。在设计者的眼中，要让“设计”的固有观念回到“空间”乃至“艺术”，打破原有陈旧的观念，打破元素的固有限制，在尊重空间内在灵魂的基础上去探求每个空间自身的个性，这才是对个性的真正到达，才是设计从共性到个性的真正升华。

To Create unique personality space environment is a common pursuit of every interior designers, but personality is not the simple sum of the elements such as materials, furniture, fabric and pile can achieve, if you abandon the internal structure, body building blocks and the spatial connotation, recessive understanding and perception, Then personality will become the wood without root, water without sources.

In the case of this design, designers pay more attention to the expression of commonness, start with respecting building inner spirit, using has consistency and regularity of the express way to deal with the block space relationship, convergent, light and shadow relationship, using the vertical elevation design, chunk face metope shop and concise furniture furnishings, mining building its own charm, restore natural living space - "home" concept. At the same time, according to the background, the designer put the space itself and the place together, by contrast, harmonious and unified design methods such as the second creation, through the positioning of furniture style, the choice of accessories and decoration material the simple sense of the dominant elements to shape the distinctive temperament that belong to this space.

Such as dining-room metope of assembled solid silver mirror decoration, sitting room background wall, as well as in the rest area with southeast Asia elements of wall coverings, the concise pure straight line of furniture and spatial layout on the vertical and horizontal piece with the interlock, unified the space rigid frame style. And simple and elegant fabric inside the sitting room and modern furniture permeate a relaxed sense of quality, strong contrast and plain on colour tone to cater to the human household style of quiet space, invigorative. These design elements are inseparable, and space one integrated mass, make the space decoration and design has the uniqueness. In the eyes of the designer, let the ideas of "design" to "space" and "art", breaking the original old ideas, break the inherent limitation of elements, to respect the basis of the inner soul of space go up to explore every space has its own personality, this is the real reach of the individuality, is the real sublimation of design from the general to the individual.

9850
1050
2700
2850
3250
写字台
厨房
儿童房
主卧
卫生间
3400
7200
1850
1950
客厅
餐厅
榻榻米
3400
7200
3800
1150
8725
9875

平面布置图

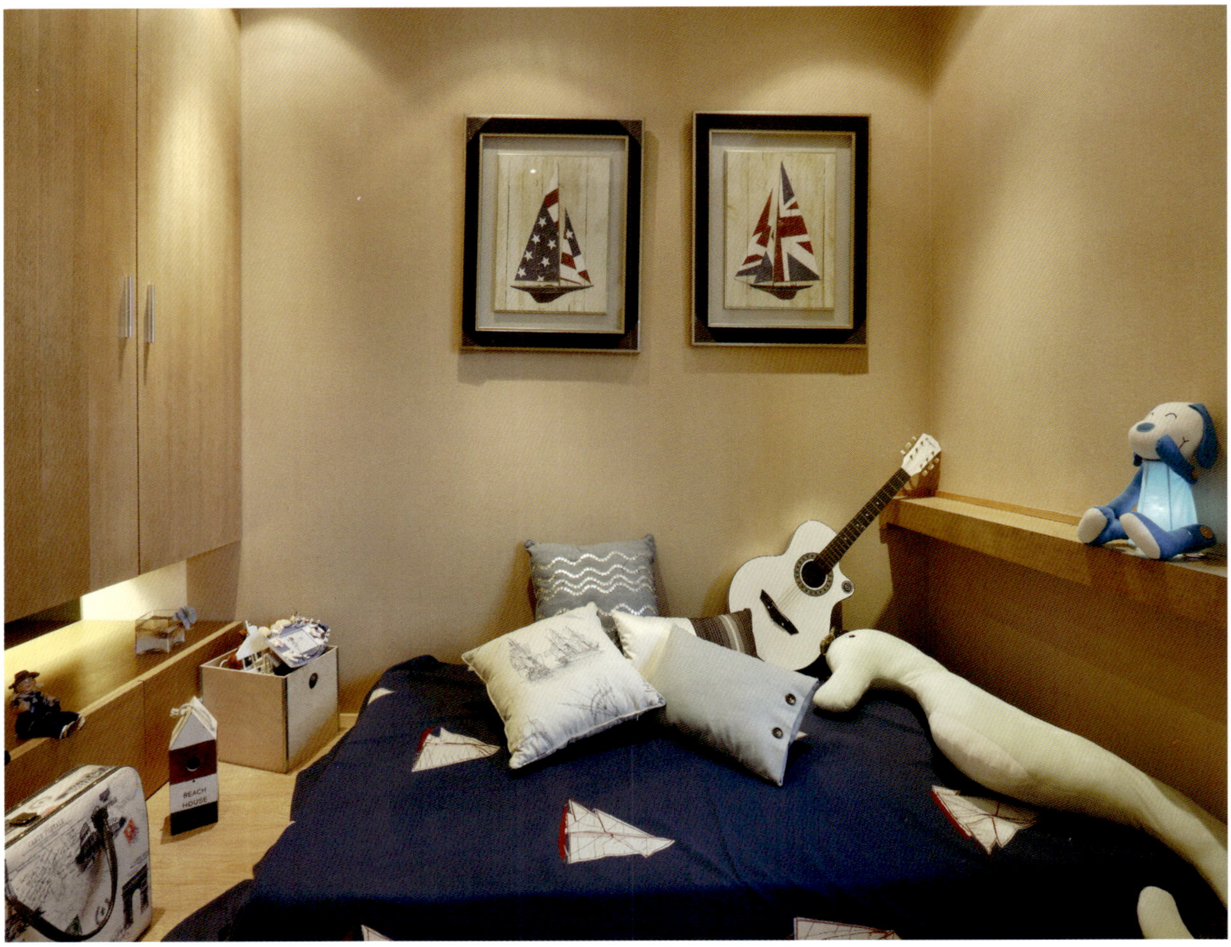

14

QINHUANGDAO GOLDEN COAST SEA BROAD MANSION

秦皇岛黄金海岸海阔海公馆

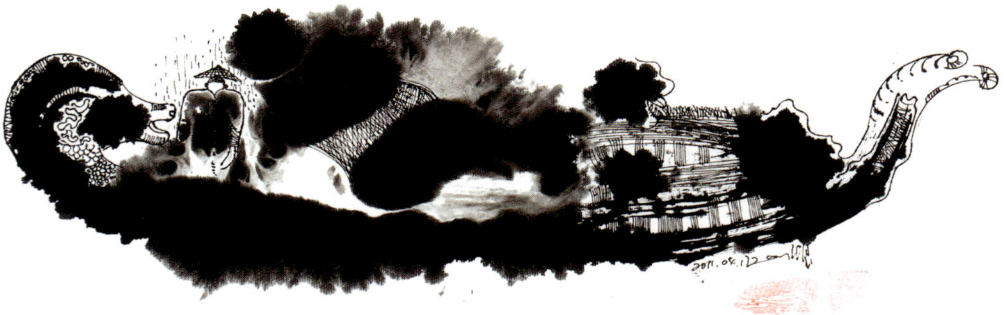

Project name: Qinhuangdao Golden Coast Sea Broad Mansion
Developer: HaiKuo Real Estate Development co., Ltd
Construction area: 1200 square meters
Using materials: cherry wood veneer, archaize brick, black and white, cream-colored stone, wood, grain coating, senior wallpaper, real wood floor
Location of project: Qinhuangdao
Design time: in December 2011

项目名称：秦皇岛黄金海岸海阔海公馆
开发商：海阔房地产开发有限公司
建筑面积：1200 m^2
使用物料：樱桃木饰面、仿古砖、黑白根、米黄石材、颗粒涂料、木雕花、高级壁纸、实木地板
项目地点：河北秦皇岛
设计时间：2011年12月

黄金海岸海阔海公馆定位为托斯卡纳风格，以托斯卡纳的异域元素为着眼点，通过严谨对称的布局形式以及优美的线条来丰富整个空间的装饰效果，通过大气、尊贵、典雅的空间，展现休闲、淡定、美丽的品质生活。

设计师主要通过形体、材料及色彩对比以及丰富的块面层次感建立内部空间的关系。入口处呈现在眼前恢宏大气的异域风情，简洁而棱角分明的吊顶让整个场景充满了张力。精致的吊灯去除了笨重的感觉，视觉上没有任何压抑感。此项细节设计充分考虑了人的视觉心理学，同时也着重表现了托斯卡纳的原生态，与主题进行了完美的呼应。大面积的拱形落地窗将自然光照运用得淋漓尽致，金色阳光的托斯卡纳情调又一次喷薄而出。场景的生命力、文化底蕴则由神秘的深色地砖走边静静地释放着。拱形门中镶嵌着精心设计的深木色雕花，别具匠心的功能隔断，将两个独立的空间完美地结合。

二楼过道顶部深色的木饰面吊顶结合暖色的灯光，洋溢着意大利葡萄酒的感觉。木饰面的拼凑留下的接缝好似葡萄酒的木桶纹理，这不仅仅是单纯的审美，更是一种生活方式的体现。设计师将这些关乎自然本质的元素，巧妙地融合在一起，带给我们一场视觉的盛宴、生活的饕餮之旅。

The Golden Coast Sea Broad Mansion is located at the Tuscan style, to Tuscany on exotic elements, through the strict symmetrical layout forms and graceful lines to enrich the adornment effect of whole space, through the space atmosphere, noble, elegant, show leisure, calm and beautiful quality life.

Stylist is mainly through the form, materials and color contrast and rich administrative levels to establish internal space area. From the entrance to the present are unselfish generosity of different region amorous feelings, the condole top of concise and angular let the scene full of tension. In addition to the delicate chandeliers heavy feeling, without any hint of depressive feeling on the vision. The detail design fully consider the person's visual psychology, but also shows the native Tuscan emphatically, and subject to the perfect echo. The arched window of large area use natural light to get incisively and vividly, Tuscan sentiment of golden sunlight, the vitality of the scene, the floor tile of the culture by the dark and mysterious release silently walk. Arched door decorated with elaborate design in deep color of carve patterns or designs on woodwork, as the function partition, the space of two independent perfect combination.

On the second floor corridor at the top of the dark wood veneer condole carries on the combination of warm color, which is light and permeated with the feeling of Italian wine. Wood decorative surface piece left seam like wine barrel texture, it is not just a simple aesthetic, but also a way of life. Designers will combine the nature of natural elements, skilfully fuses in together, brings us a visual feast, dramatic journey of life.

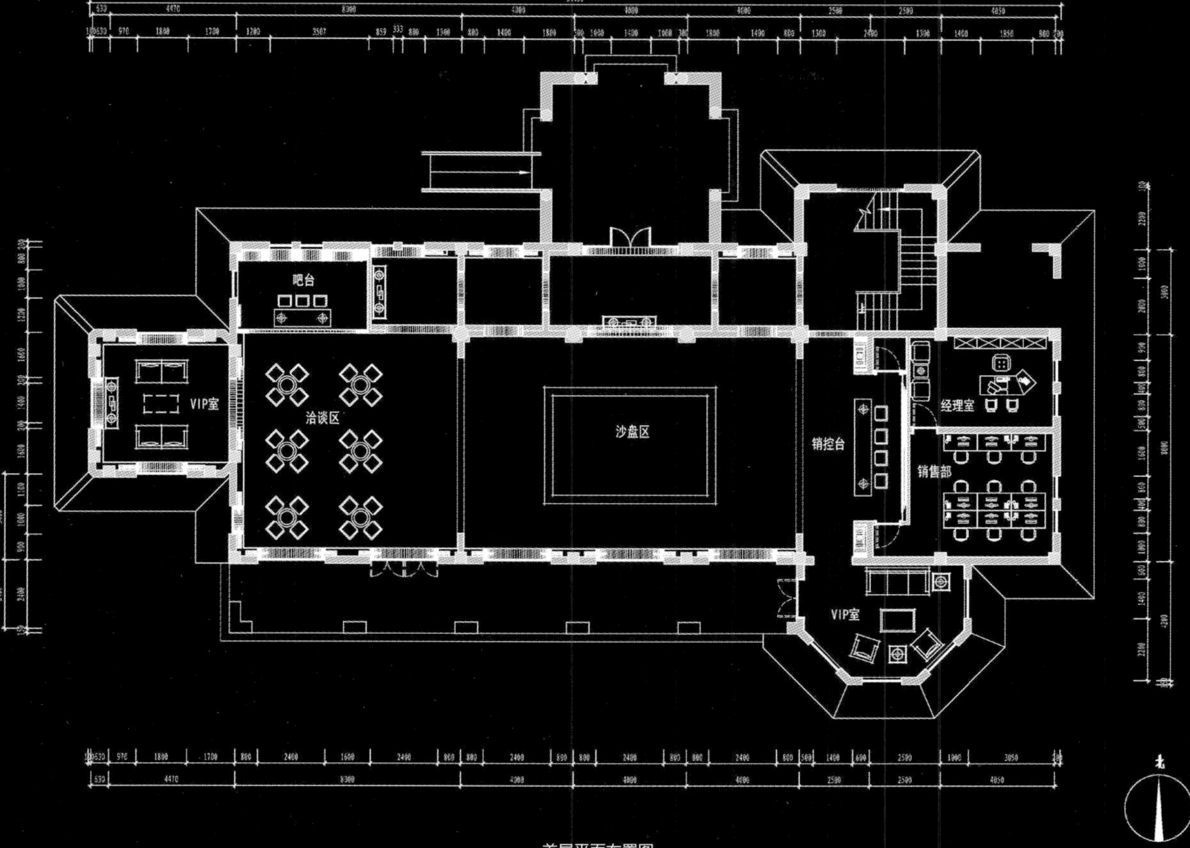

首层平面布置图

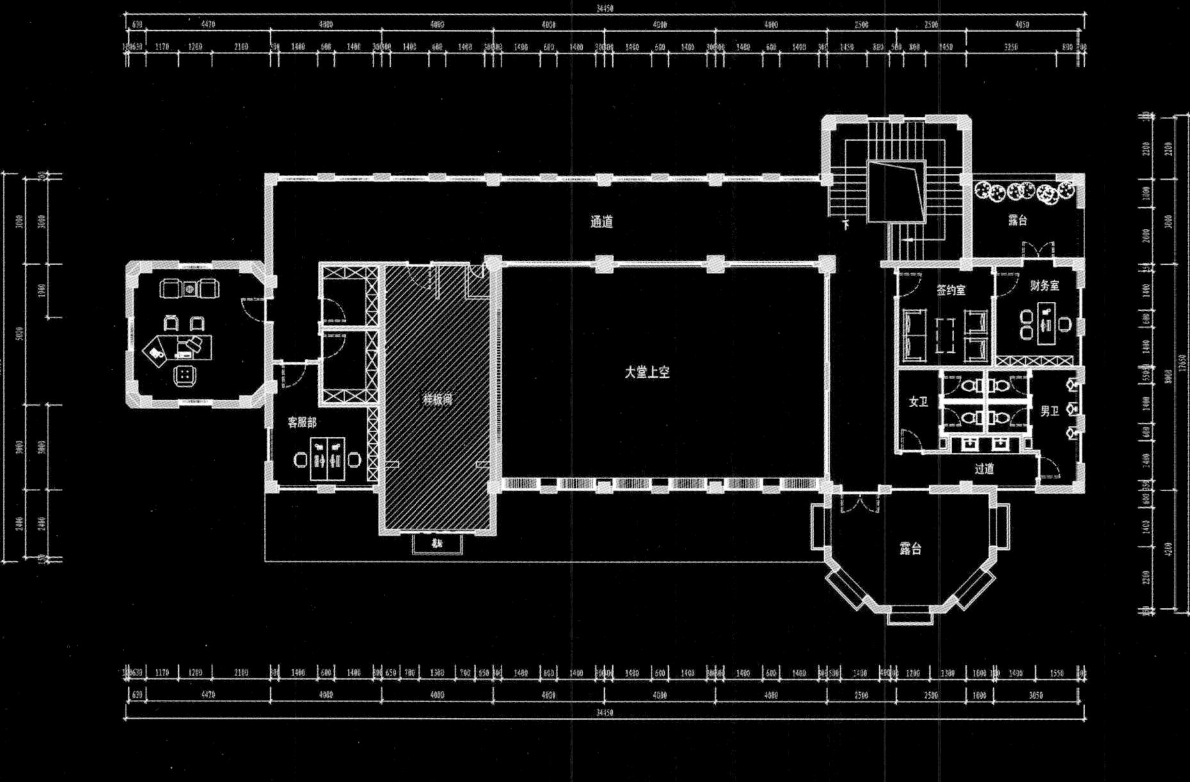

二层平面布置图

海公馆

DREAM
公馆
假日新主张
Apartments

15

CHONGQING CHANGJIAHUI C

重庆长嘉汇C户型样板间

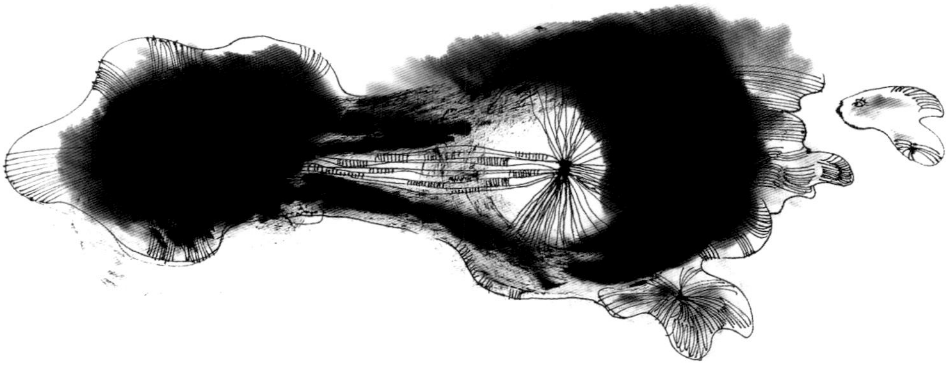

Project name: Chongqing Changjiahui C
Real estate & investment real estate developers: Hong Kong
Construction area: 132 square meters
Using materials: white scholars, senior wallpaper, leather, silver white dragon, black gold flower stone, black mirror, silver mirror, advanced coatings, high solid mu fu joins a floor board
Location of project: Chongqing
Design time: in June 2012

项目名称： 重庆长嘉汇C户型样板间
开发商： 香港置地&招商地产
建筑面积： 132 m^2
使用物料： 雅士白、高级壁纸、皮革、银白龙、黑金花石材、黑镜、银镜、高级涂料、高级实木复合地板
项目地点： 重庆
设计时间： 2012年6月

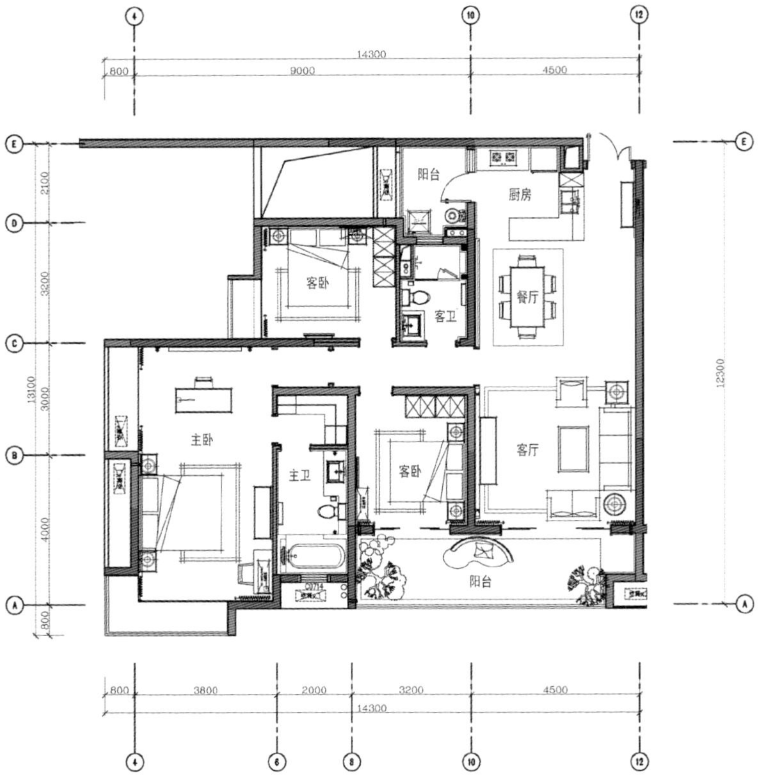

平面

本案整体设计以古典线条的层次加上现代手法，让线条更加立体而不复杂，使空间呈现出挑高而精致的延伸感。整体色彩以白色系为主轴，更让人有种极致奢华的美感。从人文精神的概念出发，强调生活与空间的巧妙互动，唯美古典，豪情意气，设计感赋予其中。作为大户型空间，本案不但具备其通常意义上的豪华贵气，更运用各种设计语汇，细致入微。淡雅清爽的色彩，大体量的家具与陈设配饰，将阔大的空间布置得有血有肉，身形具备，整个空间表现出宽敞而又饱满的不凡气势。

新古典讲究气度，“大气”是基本元素，但“细微”事物更藏着文化与工艺的精华。雕花、地面拼花图案都蕴藏着欧洲贵族的徽印，丰富了空间的层次，也拉近了人与艺术的距离。

现代感强烈的车边银镜茶几，底下是肌理感强烈的花色地毯。延伸到电视背景墙，用厚重的石材电视背景墙将这个场景压住，使其在现代感与古朴质感中驻足。整个空间在银镜的镜面反射中，新古典与现代的浪漫情怀再一次升华。

主卧中大胆运用粗犷的欧式实木纹理，将卧室的温馨感提炼出来。奢华的双人床带着一丝生活的浪漫情趣。宽敞的书房空间，进一步提升了主人的人文情怀和生活质量。

The overall design of the case with the level of the classic lines and modern technique, make the line more stereoscopic and incomplex, to make the space presents relative high extension and delicate feeling. The overall colour with white department for spindle, more let a person have a luxurious aesthetic feeling. Starting from the concept of humanism, emphasizing the clever interactive life and space, the case of beautiful, classic, enthusiastic spirit and design factors exists. As a large family of space, the case not only with its usual sense of the luxury expensive nature, use all kinds of design languages, more nuanced. The color of quietly elegant and relaxed, a high volume of furniture and furnishings of the large space layout of flesh and blood, body, whole space show the spacious situation and full of momentum.

New classical exquisite bearing,. "Atmosphere" is the basic element, but "details" things hides the essence of the culture and technology. Carve patterns or designs on woodwork, ground pattern spelling a flower is to contain the European aristocrats badge printing, enrich the levels of the space, and close to the people and art.

Under the car side silver mirror tea table, contemporary feeling strong texture is strong color carpet. Extends to the TV setting wall, with a heavy stone TV setting wall will be put, which make the modern and ancient texture mixed and stop for a while. The whole space in the silver mirror reflection, to improve the level of the new classical and modern romantic feelings.

The main bedroom is advocated by the rough European-style solid wood texture, which let the bedroom full of comfort. Luxurious double bed brings a little romantic side of life. Spacious study room, further to enhance the feelings and life quality of the master.

16

TIANJIN SCIENCE AND TECHNOLOGY SQUARE FLOOR

天津科技广场售楼处

Project name: Tianjin Science and Technology Square Floor
Developers: Wanhe Real Estate
Construction area: 4000 square meters
Using material: black iron ash wood veneer, wood stone, Eurasian wood grain stone, black mirror steel, senior wallpaper, leather, high quality hard box, deep brown, senior paintings, silver mirror, senior Jin Shiji cream-colored stone, solid real wood floor board
Project location: Tianjin
Design time: in October 2011

项目名称：天津科技广场售楼处
开发商：万和地产
建筑面积：4000 m^2
使用物料：黑铁木饰面、灰木纹石材、欧亚木纹石材、黑镜钢、高级壁纸、皮革、优质硬包、深杭啡、高级涂料、银镜、金世纪米黄石材、高级实木复合地板
项目地点：天津
设计时间：2011年10月

本案空间以现代简约的手法、用干练流畅的线条完成空间立面的处理，整个空间层次分明、远近有序，给予来客一种优雅愉悦的感受。色彩与灯光的运用，铺展开一幅绚丽、动感时尚画面。

大量银镜和茶镜的使用为整个环境的视野层次感做了进一步提升。区域沙盘的科技含量将现代感完美演绎。大沙盘上空的PVC版独特造型在灯光的烘托下显得梦幻绚烂，和谐地融入整个场景中。沙盘背景墙上，鲜活的大红色将场景生命力恰到好处地焕发出来。

整体功能分区明确，以墙面为展示功能区，结合单体模型，整体宣传十分到位。过道不同色彩的石材拼铺像跃动的琴键跳跃在整个画面之中。在设计主题的营造上，重在以不同强弱的镜面反射统合空间。欧亚木纹铺装的地面和墙面在红色造型墙的映衬下，延续了空间的动感。

The file space use the contemporary and contracted style, deal with the processing of spatial elevation by the able and fluent line, the whole space is distinct, and orderly, to give visitors a sense of elegant and pleasant. The introduction of the color and light, spread a flowery, dynamic fashion picture.

A large number of silver mirror and the use of tea glass take the whole environmental view further, which enhance the administrative levels. The modern science of the sand area is perfectly deduced. PVC version of distinctive modeling over the big sand area under the lamplight foil looks dreamy and harmoniously from the scene. The setting wall of sand table, vivid red scene displayed properly on the scene.

On the design theme of the construction, mainly on the mirror which is integrated with space and with different strength. The floor borad and wall of Eurasian wood shop extend the dynamic feelings under the red modeling wall background.

一层平面布置图

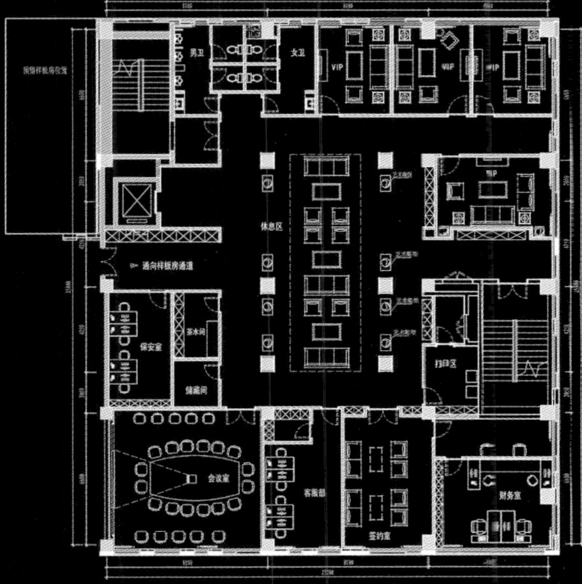

二层平面布置图

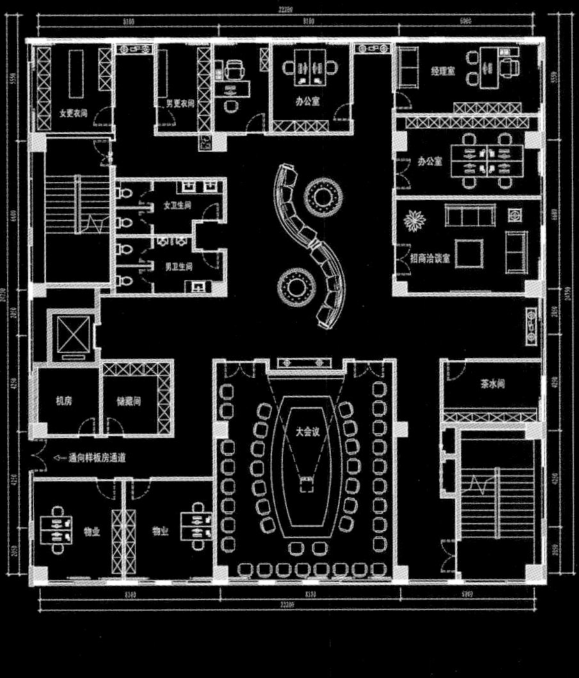

三层平面布置图

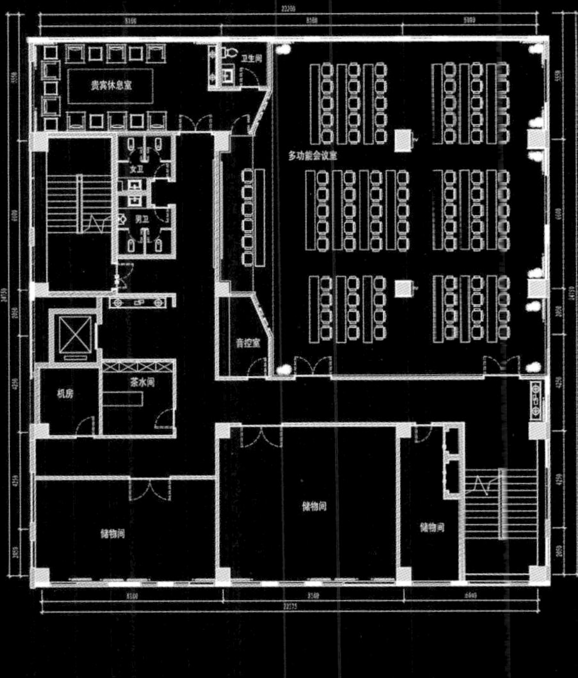

四层平面布置图

科技
广场
TECHNOLOGY
P L A Z A

17

BEIJING GUANSHANYUE A AGAINST VILLA MODEL HOUSE

北京观山悦A反别墅样板房

Project name: Beijing Guanshanyue A against villa model house
Developers: Beijing Science Park Construction (Group) co., Ltd
Construction area: 470 square meters
Use material: new sago stone, wood veneer, senior wallpaper, tropical rain forest, black golden flower, silver mirror, senior paintings, silver foil, senior real wood floor, solid floor board
Project location: Beijing
Design time: in March 2012

项目名称： 北京观山悦A反别墅样板房
开发商： 北京科技园建设(集团)股份有限公司
建筑面积： 470 m^2
使用物料： 新西米石材、木饰面、高级壁纸、热带雨林、黑金花、银镜、高级涂料、银箔、高级实木复合地板、实木地板
项目地点： 北京
设计时间： 2012年3月

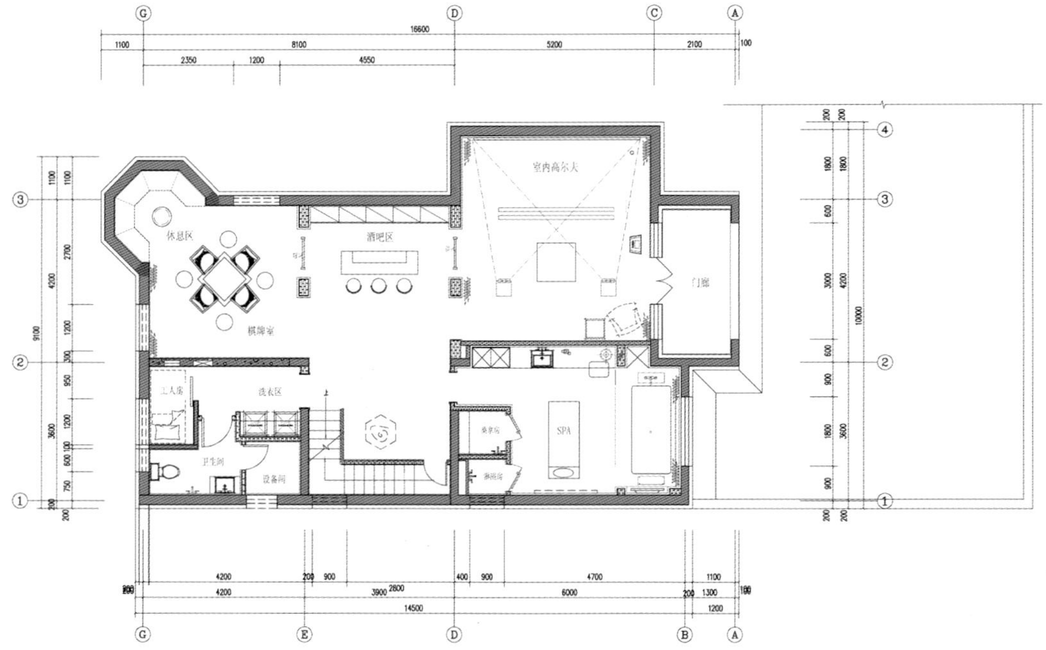

负一层平面布置图

本案的风格特点是原始自然、色泽鲜艳、崇尚手工。在设计上，凝练的直线条，使空间看上去沉稳干练。对称的木作造型，营造出浓郁的热带风情，散发着浓郁的自然气息。在家具配置上，选用了实木家具，力求表现实木的自然原始之美，线条简约凝练，更具舒适性。细节处点缀东南亚风格装饰，凸显其风格特征。在布艺色调的选用上，东南亚风格标志性的炫色系列多为深色系，且在光线下会变色，在沉稳中透着一点贵气，以温馨淡雅的中性色彩为主，局部点缀艳丽的红色，自然温馨中不失热情华丽。在材质上，运用壁纸、实木、硅藻泥等，演绎原始自然的热带风情。

客厅以精致古朴为主，旧木质感的沙发配以朴素的布艺，浮雕拼铺的米黄色文化石在镂空的深色木挂版的映衬下使空间更具层次感。在配饰上，东南亚风情的饰品和色彩艳丽的抱枕衬托出客厅活跃的气氛。

红色布艺的餐椅，营造出热情洋溢的气氛。餐桌上方的雨伞状小吊灯，使人感到既创新独特，又似曾相识，温馨而自然。主卧室选用了深木色，金色丝制布料结合光线的变化，创造出内敛谦卑的奢华。主卫石材与镜子的设计，为其增加了变化。奢华既非繁杂的雕饰，更非金碧辉煌的装饰，只要充分地运用材质的特点，现代的设计也可以传达视觉与舒适的平衡。

The style characteristic of this case is the original nature, bright color, advocating manually. In terms of the design, the straight and concise line, which makes the space looks calm. The compared wooden furniture in symmetry, build a full-bodied tropical amorous feelings, sending out the rich natural breath. On the configuration, to choose the solid wood furniture, make every effort to show the natural beauty of the original of real wood, simple concise line, more comfortably. The decoration of the southeast Asian style is adorned , highlights its unique characteristic. In the choice of cloth, the color of Southeast Asian characteristics is mainly on the dark color, and under the light, it will change to other color, and show a little of luxurious space among the stable environment, mainly on the comfortable and elegant color, part of it is covered by red color, in the calm environment, you will feel elegant, and the old sofa feeling is matched with the pure cloth art. In term of the materials selection, we use the wallpaper, real wood and diatom ooze, deduce the original nature and tropical amorous feelings.

The sitting room is given priority with elegant of primitive simplicity, old woodiness sense with plain cloth art sofa, beige culture stone is on the dark wood, to make the space more administrative levels feels. On the accessories, southeast Asia amorous feelings of ornaments and colorful pillow set off the atmosphere of the sitting room is active.

Red cloth art of chair for eating, create a warm atmosphere. Mensal upper part of the umbrella shape small droplight, make the person feels both innovative, unique and familiar, warm and natural. Advocate the bedroom and choose the deep color, golden silk fabrics combine the change of the light, to create inside collect luxury of humility. Advocate defend stone material and the design of the mirror, increase the change frequency for it. Luxury is neither the multifarious carve, the resplendent and magnificent decoration, as long as you take the full use of the characteristics of the materials, the modern design can convey the balance of the visual and comfort.

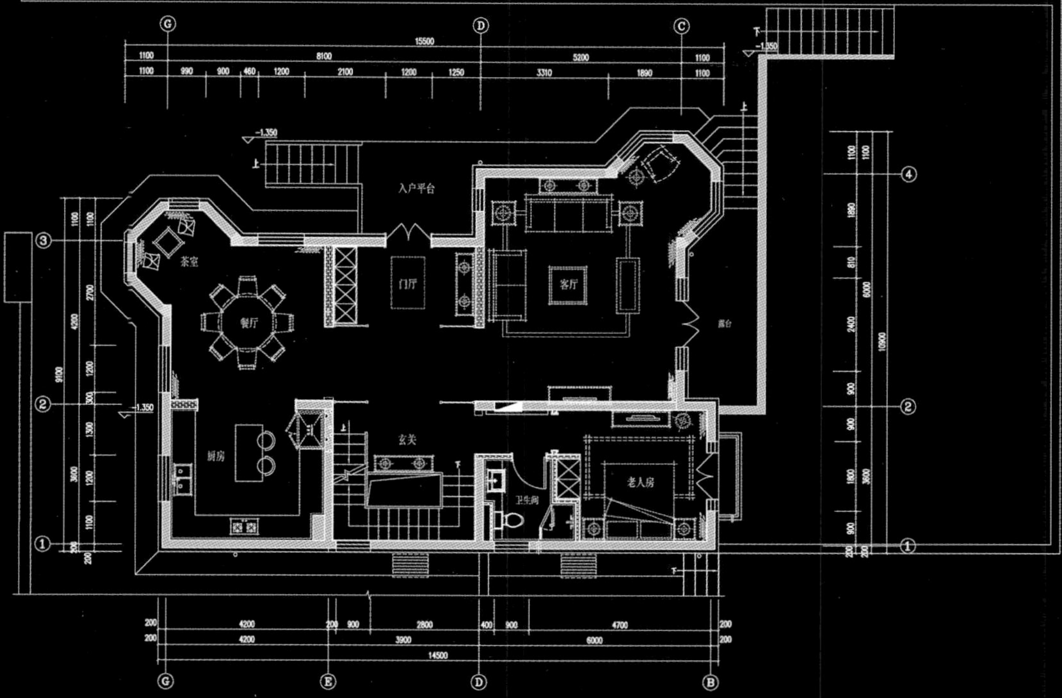

一层平面布置图

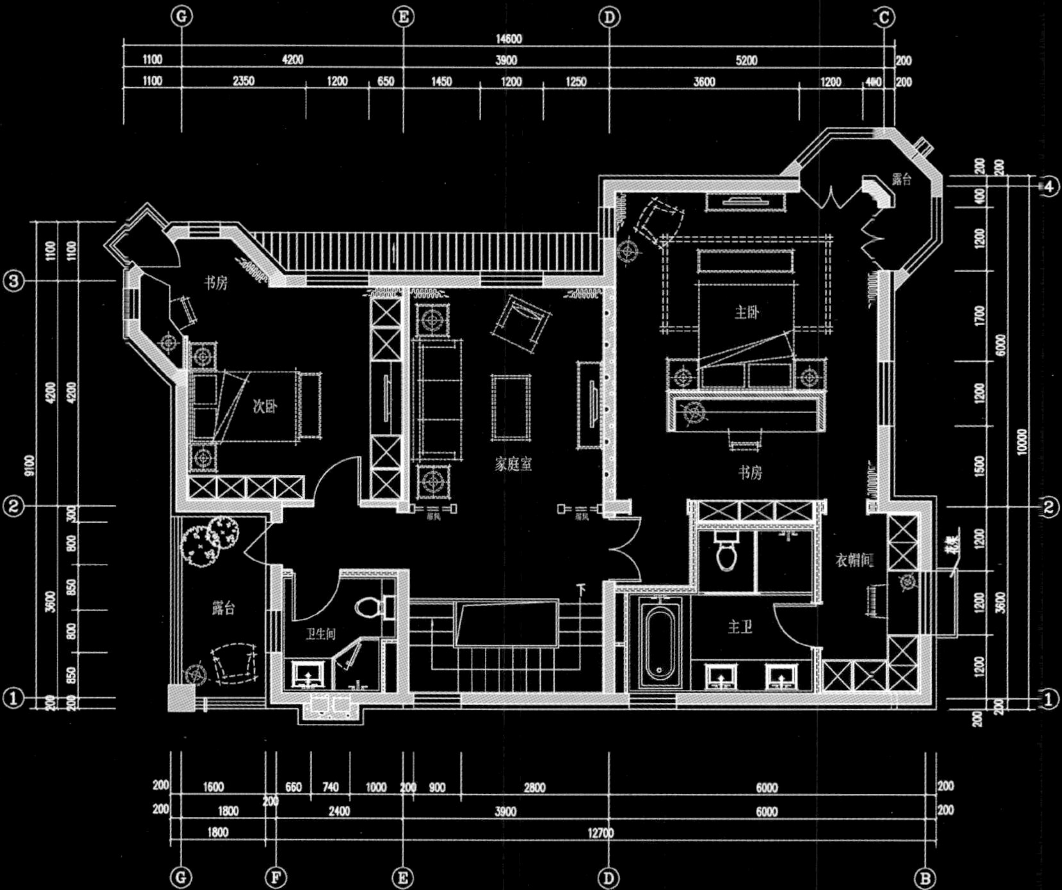

18

QINHUANGDAO DAIHESHOULING MODEL HOUSE

秦皇岛戴河首岭样板房

Project name: Qinhuangdao Daiheshouling Model House
Developers: Qinhuangdao Jinhai eal estate development co., Ltd
Construction area: 110 square meters
Using materials: particles coatings, archaize floor tile, silver foil, senior senior wallpaper, senior carpet
Location of project: Qinhuangdao
Design time: in April 2010

项目名称：秦皇岛戴河首岭样板房
开发商：秦皇岛金海房地产开发有限公司
建筑面积：110 m^2
使用物料：颗粒涂料、仿古地砖、银箔、高级壁纸、高级地毯
项目地点：河北秦皇岛
设计时间：2010年4月

本案为海景度假项目，需要营造具有强烈度假感的空间来打动客户，最终设计师为这个项目的两个样板间设计了地中海风格和托斯卡纳风格。设计上力求通过对地中海和托斯卡纳真实色彩的研究配比，还原地中海和托斯卡纳真实的人文特色与艺术积淀。

本案设计材质表达大胆粗犷，色彩运用上，大胆地使用蓝色和陶砖红色，大面积颗粒涂料的运用还原了地中海和托斯卡纳地区的风土特征，营造了特征鲜明的地中海和托斯卡纳的异域风情特点，给本项目的销售带来了强有力的视觉冲击力。

客厅地面的锈红色仿古地砖犹如托斯卡纳红色的土壤，细细品味，一丝泥土的清香袭面而来。红色的陶艺花瓶搭配橙红色的大花束，犹如纯洁的向阳花，令人想起那陶醉的金色阳光。清爽的碎花壁纸和田园风的桌布，相互诉说着托斯卡纳原生态的美好。

The case is the seaview resort project, we need to create a strong sense of holiday space to impress customers, in the end, designers put two example of the Mediterranean style and the Tuscan style. Design tries to match the two colors and restore the original view of the cultural feathers and artistic heritage in the two areas above.

In this case, the materials design expression is bold and straightforward, color is applied, the introduction of blue and ceramic brick red, and the use of large particles coatings, to create a distinctive feature of the Mediterranean and exotic characteristics of Tuscany, brought a strong visual impact to the project sales.

The sitting room ground is covered by the red rust, which is like the Tuscany red soil, carefully taste, a little scent on surface of the earth. Red pottery vases with orange red flowers, like the purity of the sunflower, reminiscent of the enhanced golden sunlight. Fresh floral wallpaper and rural wind antependium, telling each other about the Tuscan original status.

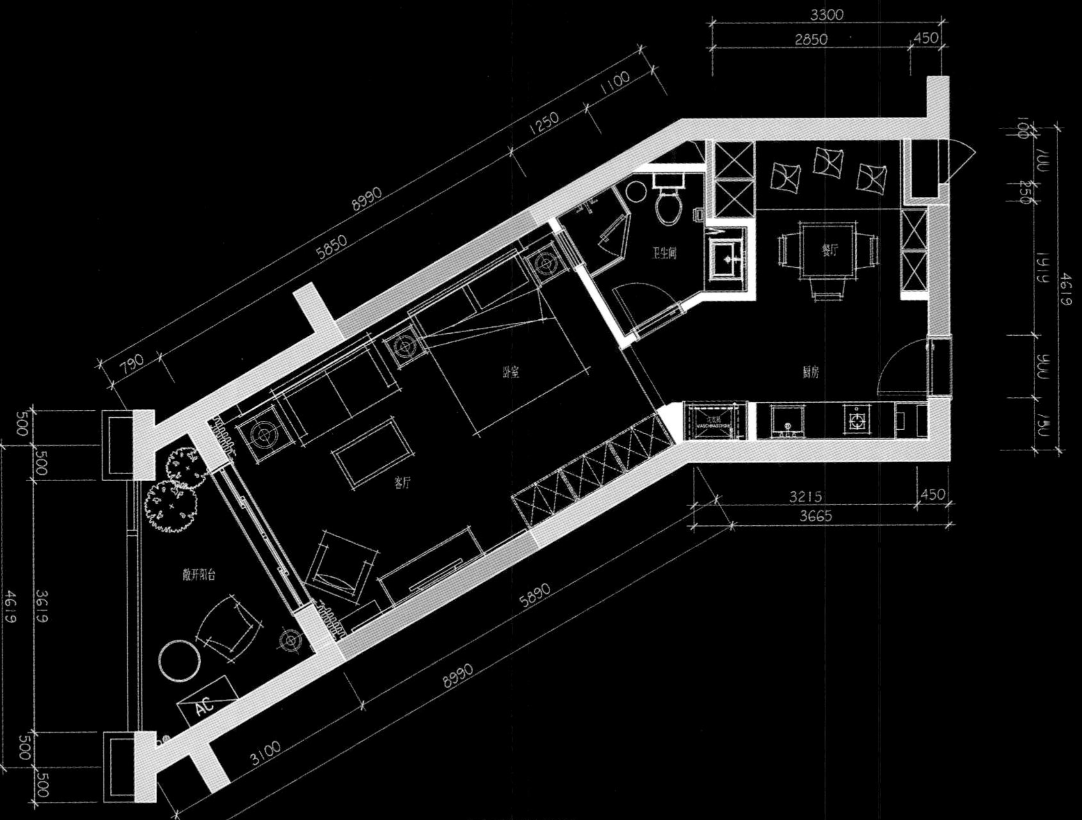
3300
2850
450
8990
5850
1250
1100
790
卫生间
餐厅
卧室
厨房
客厅
敞开阳台
AC
3215
450
3665
5890
8990
3100
4619
3619
500
500
500
500
100
700
250
1919
4619
900
750

标间平面布置图

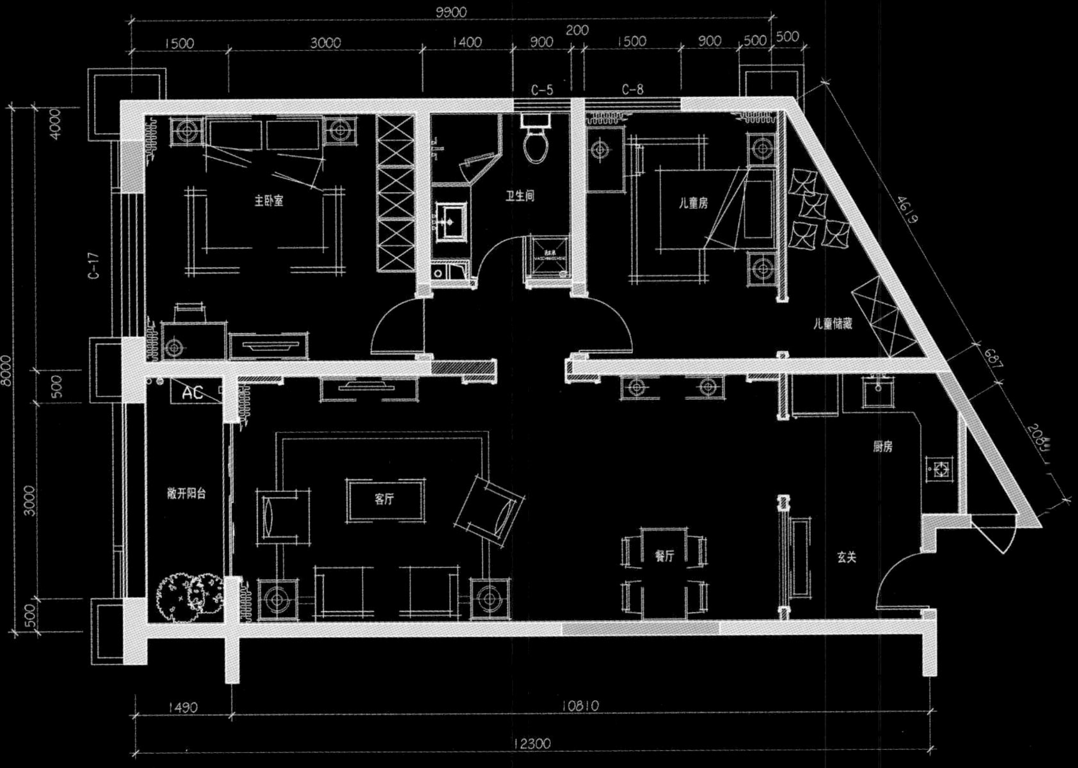
9900
1500
3000
1400
900
200
1500
900
500
500
C-5
C-8
4000
8000
500
3000
500
C-17
主卧室
卫生间
儿童房
儿童储藏
4619
687
2085
AC
敞开阳台
客厅
厨房
餐厅
玄关
1490
10810
12300

套间

With
God
things
are
ossible

Home

19

QINHUANGDAO BOYUESHAN NEW CHINESE STYLE OF MODEL HOUSE

秦皇岛铂悦山新中式样板间

Project name: Qinhuangdao Boyueshan new Chinese style of model house
Developers: Longji taihe industrial co., Ltd
Construction area: 120 square meters
Using materials: Grey wood stone, black mirror steel, senior wallpaper, leather, manual Coloured drawing or pattern, senior coatings, high solid real wood floor board
Location of project: Qinhuangdao
Design time: in May 2013

项目名称： 秦皇岛铂悦山新中式样板间
开发商： 隆基泰和实业有限公司
建筑面积： 120 m^2
使用物料： 灰木纹石材、黑镜钢、高级壁纸、皮革、手工彩绘、高级涂料、高级实木复合地板
项目地点： 河北秦皇岛
设计时间： 2013年5月

Anne of Green Gables
Anne of Green Gables

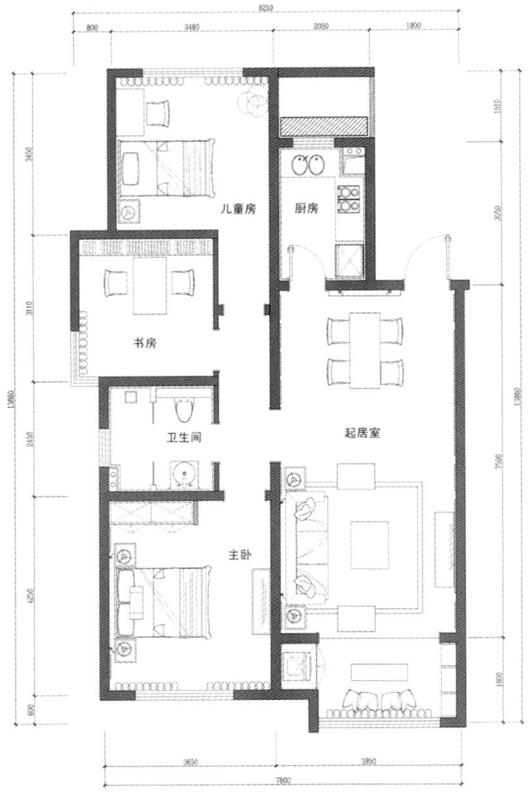

标间平面布置图

本案定位为新中式风格。通过对传统文化的认识，将现代元素和传统元素结合在一起，以现代人的审美需求，运用现代居住理念，打造出既富有传统韵味，又有当代气息的居住空间。

本案考虑现代家居的简约理念及舒适性，摈弃了很多中式的繁琐设计。但设计师颇谙中式精髓，并融合了现代的手法，打造出高雅独特、沉稳大气、具有文化底蕴的中式视觉效果。

大幅的中式手绘荷花挂画，清新淡雅，使原本狭长的空间流淌出一丝动感，围观的不仅是接天莲叶、落日楼头，更多的是一份休闲、放松的心情。设计师精心挑选的餐椅靠包和餐厅背景墙交相辉映，如同诗经中优美的音词合拍，节奏对应。

过道垭口的黑镜圈边，如中国古代宣纸般纹理的淡雅质感，是刚与柔、古朴与现代的完美交融。纵观整个场景的色彩，如同荷花般舒卷自然，充满人文关怀。窗帘的色彩有如荷花深处的根，灵感顿现的设计师在客厅的主要区域运用大面积的灰木纹，背后打上灯带，石材的质感在灯光和手绘画的衬托下，如莲亭亭，似水温润。

The location is the new Chinese style in the case. Through the understanding of traditional culture, modern elements and traditional elements are combined together, with the modern's aesthetic demand, using the modern living concepts, to create a rich and conventional flavor, and also have the contemporary factors in the living space.

This case considers the contracted concept and comfort, abandon many Chinese style design. But the designer have a good knowledge of the essence of the Chinese tradition, and also integrate the modern technologies, to create elegant and unique, composed of atmosphere, and there is a cultural charm of Chinese visual effect.

A picture of Chinese hand painted , pure and fresh quietly elegant, make originally narrow space flowing out of a dynamic, onlookers, which is not only the next day, the setting Sun is more of a recreational, relaxed mood. Designers selected chair on package and dinning -room setting wall hand in photograph reflection, like a beautiful sound word in the book of songs in tune, match the rhythm.

Corridor black mirror ring side of the pass, like the ancient Chinese paper, which the texture of quietly elegant texture, is perfect blend of a firm with soft, ancient and modern times. Throughout the whole scene color, back and forth like the natural, full of humanistic care. The color of the curtain is like the root of lotus, then the inspiration will occur to the designer, and in the sitting room of ash wood grain, behind the lamp belt, stone texture in lights and hand painting, such as the graceful lotus, like warm water.

20

RUNDIQINGYUN NEW CLASSIC MODEL HOUSE ROOM

润地青云新古典样板间

Project name: Rundiqingyun New Classic Model House Room
Developers: Rundi Real Estate
Construction area: 150 square meters
Using material: Silver mirror, ash wood, Anna cream-colored stone, cream-colored, Aegean grey stone, deep brown, black mirror, ebony facing, senior paintings, senior carpet
Location of project: Qinhuangdao
Design time: in March 2012

项目名称： 润地青云新古典样板间
开发商： 润地地产
建筑面积： 150 m^2
使用物料： 银镜、灰木纹、莎安娜米黄石材、金世纪米黄、爱琴海灰石材、深杭啡、黑镜、黑檀木饰面、高级涂料、高级地毯
项目地点： 河北秦皇岛
设计时间： 2012年3月

本案设计定位为时尚新古典风格。由色彩带动空间的灵动，用材质雕刻文化的底蕴。唯美的细节处理，华丽的时尚元素都将贵族气息推向了极致；玻璃、花艺、挂画等饰品的巧妙搭配，体现贵族的奢华，同时又展现出别具一格的时尚潮流魅力。

色彩上，使用白色、蓝绿色、黑白灰等色调。少量黄蓝色糅合，使色彩看起来明亮、大方，整个空间给人以开放、宽容的非凡气度，丝毫不显局促。通过设计师的巧妙设计，整体空间闪亮华丽，奢华中洋溢着青春的格调，尊贵中散发别具一格的魅力。

材质上，尽量保留了原生态的纹理与质感。从整体到局部，无不精雕细琢，一丝不苟。传统元素加上现代工艺，打造出舒适、尊贵的品质，令人感受到典雅的历史痕迹与浑厚的文化底蕴。

The position of the case is the classical style, driven by the color space, to show the dynamic state, and carve out cultural background material. Beautiful details are processing, luxuriant fashionable element is pushed to the highest level; Glass, flower art, collocation, which reflect the luxury of nobles, and show a unique fashion charm at the same time.

In terms of color, to use the white, blue, black and white colors. Mix a small amount of yellow and blue factors, to make the color look bright, generous,and make the whole space full of openness, tolerance, and no hurry inside the environment. Through the careful design of the designer, the whole space is full of bright factors, and young factors are among the luxuriant situation, send out a sense of unique charming status.

In terms of materials, try to keep the original texture and quality. From the overall to local area, all carved and meticulous. Traditional elements add the modern technology create comfortable, noble quality , and to feel elegant history and rich culture.

THE HOTEL BOOK
Classical Culture
Classical Culture
Furniture culture
ROCKY
ROCKY
Arletta
Fieramilano
Expo Express
Classical Culture
THE HOTEL BOOK
THE HOTEL BOOK
olivia

21

QINHUANGDAO BOYUESHAN MODERN LUXURY MODEL ROOM

秦皇岛铂悦山现代奢华样板间

Project name: Qinhuangdao Boyueshan modern luxury model room
Developers: Longji taihe industrial co., Ltd
Construction area: 110 square meters
Use material: wood veneer, Cinderella white stone, stone, senior silver mirror, black mirror, wallpaper, leather, black and white root, advanced solid real wood floor board
Location of project: Tangshan
Design time: in March 2013

项目名称： 秦皇岛铂悦山现代奢华样板间
开发商： 隆基泰和实业有限公司
建筑面积： 110 m^2
使用物料： 木饰面、雅士白石材、灰姑娘石材、银镜、黑镜、高级壁纸、皮革、黑白根、高级实木复合地板
项目地点： 河北唐山
设计时间： 2013年3月

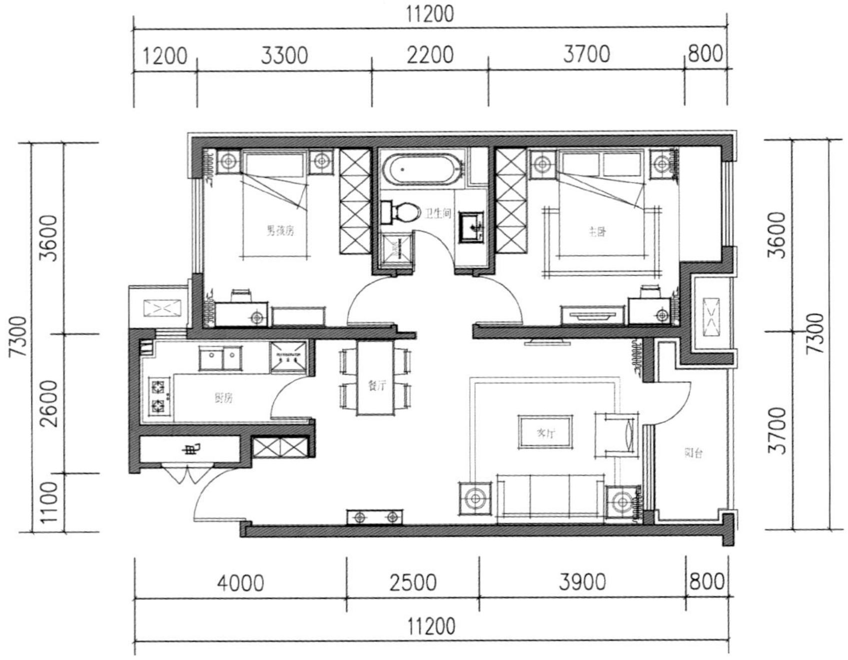

套间

本案定位为现代奢华风格，设计师采用非传统的混合、叠加等设计手法，通过优雅简洁的线条和大面积的色块对比，演绎出集传统与现代、融古典与时尚于一体的居室风格。

客厅电视背景墙大面积的木饰面结合黑钢条的造型。现代感的菱角和自然古朴的木饰面交错拼合。对应的沙发背景墙则与细腻的米白色硬包形成强烈的对比，使原本较为狭长的空间错落有致，奏出超凡脱俗的时尚节拍。

浅灰色的沙发，黑钢旧木结合的电视背景墙，低调的主卧双人床，造型简洁，没有任何多余装饰。简洁的线条通过优质的材料勾勒，倍显质感。独树一帜的结构，加上精湛的工艺，优质的材料性能，精心的色彩配置，使传统的典雅与现代的新颖相融合，创造出优美奢华的空间。

This case focus on modern luxurious style, and he designers adopt the unconventional design methods, such as mixing, superimposed by elegant lines and a large area of color piece contrast, deducing a set of traditional and modern, combining the classical and fashion factors.

The TV setting wall of sitting room is a large area of he modelling of wood veneer, combining the modern water chestnut and natural wood, corresponding to the sofa seeting wall with exquisite white hard package, which make original fashion full of space, and there is a huge fashion trend inside the sitting room.

The sofa of light grey, black steel combined with TV setting wall of old wood, low-key master bedroom with double bed, modelling concise, no excess decoration. Concise line, through be being drawn the outline of the high quality material times texture. Unique structure, combined with superb technology, high quality material, elaborating color configuration, which makes the traditional elegance and modern novel fusion, in order to create the elegant luxury of space.

22

QNHUANGDAO BOYUESHAN CONTEMPORARY AND CONTRACTED MODEL HOUSE

秦皇岛铂悦山现代简约样板房

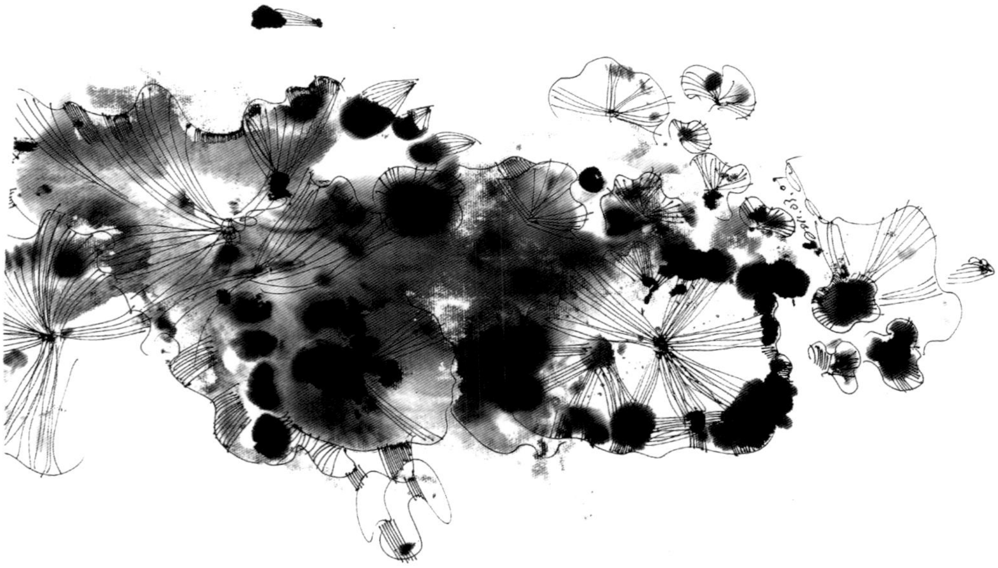

Project name: Qnhuangdao Boyueshan contemporary and contracted model House
Developers: Longji taihe industrial co., Ltd
Construction area: 120 square meters
Using materials: wood veneer, white stone, Cinderella, senior silver mirror, black mirror, wallpaper, leather, black and white root, advanced coatings, high solid real wood floor board
Location of project: Tangshan
Design time: in January 2013

项目名称：秦皇岛铂悦山现代简约样板房
开发商：隆基泰和实业有限公司
建筑面积：120 m^2
使用物料：木饰面、雅士白石材、灰姑娘、银镜、黑镜、高级壁纸、皮革、黑白根、高级涂料、高级实木复合地板
项目地点：河北唐山
设计时间：2013 年 1 月

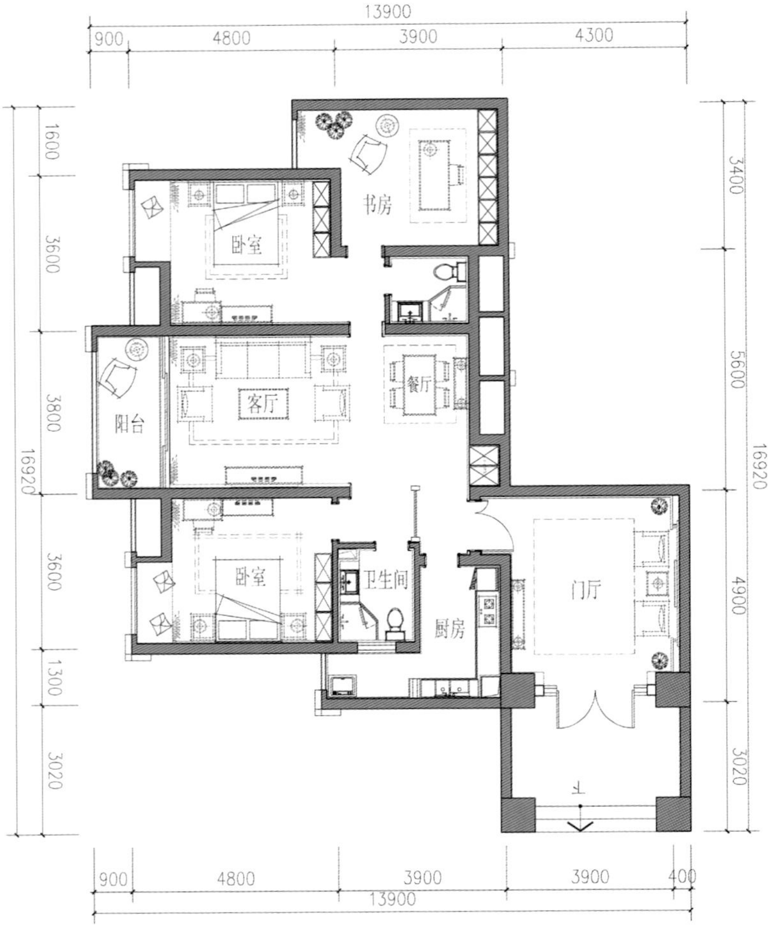

套间

本案设计师秉承简约时尚的现代风格，在设计上既具有历史的延续性，又不拘泥于传统的思维方式，将古典与现代、传统与时尚的元素兼容并蓄，形成有力量但不生硬、有活力但不稚嫩的空间风格。

本案采用大量的纯色块结合大量黑钢线条，意图营造出简约纯粹、富有质感的品质生活空间。设计师利用多种不同的材质组合空间，利用多样的光影进行反射，光亮的、暗淡的、华丽的、古朴的、平滑的、粗糙的，相互穿插对比，使简约的线条变得灵动且更有内容。

客厅整体使用了较为纯粹的颜色。朴实无华的地面，大气从容的布艺纹理。过道垭口处黑镜反射的绿色荷叶般的光影。电视背景墙的红色壁灯、沙发上的红色靠包、卧室床头背景墙的红色剪贴画产生共鸣，却又和素雅的绿色产生鲜明的对比。大红与素绿，在设计师的巧妙安排下，不仅没有丝毫冲突，只觉接天莲叶、映日荷花，一派清新自然、落落大方的美好景象。

The stylist in the case adheres to the contracted and fashionable modern style, in terms of the design, not only have the continuity of the history, but the designer thinks outside of the box, which mix the ancient and modern factors, blend them and take advantage, to form a powerful but not stiff, energetic but naive space style.

This case introduces a large number of pure color, to create a simple and abundant quality life. Designers take advantages of different materials combination space,to use a variety of light and shadow of reflection, light, dark, luxuriant, of primitive simplicity, smooth, rought, compared with each other, make the simple lines become dynamic and more content.

The whole sitting room use a relatively pure color. The plain ground, atmosphere with leisure fabric texture. Corridor pass black mirror reflection of light green lotus leaf. TV setting wall of red wall lamp, to sofa of red package, the setting wall of bedroom, to have common sound, but compare with the pure green factor. Red and green, under the careful arrangement of the designer, not only have no conflict, only feel lotus, fresh and natural feeling, graceful scenery show in this case.

張雲 Zhang Yun

宁缺毋滥做设计　轻松慵懒过生活！
这一路走来……

离上一次整理、出版作品已经有七、八年时间了，后来一直想把作品再汇总、集结，回馈给支持我的朋友，但是这个念头，又一次次地被自己否定——也许还是对设计过于苛刻、对完美过于执著，所以再版的时间，一拖再拖。这次在张怀的紧追力推下，新书出炉，还要求我这个YLH设计总监必须得说上几句。

这对我来说无异于一个重拾碎片的过程。回顾每一个项目的设计，全都历历在目，记忆犹新。然而提起笔，脑海中不断有旧忆来袭，新的火花又噼啪作响，我时顿时续，进展缓慢。好吧，我承认，这么多年过去，我依然只会产生碎片而没有学会整理。但我马上安慰自己说，如果我学会了整理，也许就不会产生那么多更好的碎片。

事实上，设计的辩证也是如此，设计的魅力亦在于此。“美”总是相对而言的，只有人规定窗户台高是900，没有人规定客厅永远是要装吊灯。随着社会的发展，环境在变化，人们的思维在变化，人们理想的空间也会随之变化。什么才是好的设计？简单的四个字：好看，好用。然而越是简单地追求，越是难以实现。所以我从不刻意地去计划某种空间效果，我常常放任自己的思维碎片，动不动就迸发，时不时升华一下，然后美其名曰：“灵感”。

从毕业到现在，已经15年。做了这么多年设计，很多客户也给了我们肯定，还有很多设计师问我设计到底该怎么做？设计师是不是要靠灵感来发挥？凭感觉来设计？所以设计师要有很多灵感？是不是要有很多天赋？等等。我说都没有错，都应该具备。然而灵感总是转瞬即逝，设计师靠什么来捕捉灵感，把这些散落的思维碎片，串成别致的项链？在经年累月的沉淀之后，我可以肯定地告诉你：是爱，是源于内心深处对万物的“爱”。

这个定义听起来特俗，但这既是一个我无法否认和回避的事实，又是在经历数十年的磨砺后，一种返璞归真的领悟。市场上从来不缺乏好材料，但是常常有人把它们堆积得不伦不类；有人在电视背景墙上贴金砖，却不如孤儿寄来的土黄色明信片美。我始终相信，爱是可以传递的。一个没有爱心的人做出来的设计，只会是没有灵魂的拼凑。而用心、用爱的设计，会把我们的梦想和追求，传递到每一个置身空间的人。只要他们驻足，他们就能感受到设计师的人文关怀，感受到生活的幸福与美好。

To design with one's best, and to enjoy life in a comfortable and easy way.
This along the way...

There were seven or eight years until the last summary, during that time, I have always been thinking that re-summarizing, recondensation, and back to support my friends, but this idea, time and time again, it has been criticised by myself, maybe the design is too harsh, and to pursuing the perfect is too persistent, so the time of reprinting, has always been dragging its feet. This time, under the pushing of the Mr Huai Zhang, the new boo has been published, and asking me the project director of YLH), to say some words about the project.

It is a process of picking up pieces, holding the book, and reviewing each project design detail, which were all in the mind stored in memory. Though picking up the pen, in my mind there are huge amount of old memory, and the new sparks crackles, and for me, sometimes proceed, sometimes backwards thinking, anyway, I admit that during the past years, I still make up the pieces, and cannot learn to summarize in the whole, but I always think in the other way, if I learned that to arrange or summarize the past pieces in my memory, maybe I cannot product much more pieces in my life;.

In fact, the dialectical analysis of the design and the charm of the design is like the same way. The "Beauty" is always relative, and only the window has been defined the height of them is 900, and no rule for people to install the droplight in the sitting room. With the development of the society, and the changes in the environment, and the thinking patterns in the people's mind, and the ideal space will also vary based on the dynamic environment. And what is the best design? To be simple, good looking and easy to use. However, the more simple pursuit in the life, and the more difficult to realize. So I were not used to plan certain space effect, and I always put my thought fragments in a dynamic state, sometimes to burst,occasionally sublimation, then known as "inspiration".

From the graduation to now, there has been 15 years for designing things in life. Many clients give us the definition of the design, and other primary designers ask me that how to design essentially? Relying on the real inspiration? Or the feeling to design? So the designers must have many inspirations? And dependent on some gift? And so on. I said there are no wrong answers for you, the designers should also possess, and for the designers, what can be relied on to capture the inspiration, and to scatter the fragments in the memory, to form a chain of brilliant necklace? After many years of precipitation, I can tell you for sure, is love, is the from the deep heart and love all things in life.

The definition of the design sounds very vulgar, but it is not only a fact that I cannot deny and avoid, and after hard-working of decades of years, I have a strong feeling that back to pursuit the original nature and life of the human beings. The market have many good materials, but people always put them in a disorder way, someone put the TV setting wall with the golden bricks, but not the khaki postcard from orphans, so brilliant and remarkable memory. I always believe the love can be deliver in a way. A man does not the nature of the design, then his or her work maybe a work that has been put together. However, if you use your heart, and design of the love, then you can put your beautiful dreams into everyone in the space. As long as they stand, they will feel the humanitarian care, have the feeling of the happiness and beauty of the life

張浪 Zhang lang

我的一生一直在追寻“美”，事物为什么“美”，也许有许多书本里说高大、排列、对称、比例等，我认为这些似乎还是不够的。“美”一定有其内在的特殊的东西，这些东西也许能表现在表面，也许存在心里。有些喜欢动物的朋友提醒了我，当我不知道他们为什么喜欢动物时我认为他们被动物的美吸引了；当我们说艺术与技术结合才是美的时候，那我们需要认为技术也是美的一部分，难道不是吗；男女朋友之间谈恋爱，有句话说情人眼里出西施，婚后组织家庭其乐融融，那也是美滋滋的；也许例子很多，我觉得作为设计师，产品的造型除了事物表象之外，还有积淀的文化和历史的沉淀。总之，围绕“美”来展开要做优秀的设计师，还要有优秀的人格才是最美的。

Pursuing the real beauty is the goal of my life, why the beauty exists in the world,maybe some books say something like that "tall, arrangement, symmetry, proportion and so on" is representatives of the beauty. "Beauty"must have its inherent special things, these things may be able to be shown on the surface, perhaps exists in your heart. Some friends who like the animals remind me, when I don't know why they are fond of animals, because they are deeply attracted by the beauty of the animals at that time; When we say that combining art and technology is the real beauty, then we need to consider the technology is part of beauty, isn't it? Love between male and female, an old saying that "the eyes of beholders will come out Xishi",after marriage, the whole family feel happy, which is full of fun in life; Perhaps many examples happen, the point I would say that the modeling of products takes apart from the surface of the things, more importantly is the accumulation of the culture and the precipitation of history. Therefore, around the "beauty" there is a need to be a brilliant designer, and good personality is the most beautiful.

張怀 **Zhang Huai**

经过近一年的筹备，新书终于付梓，这期间的艰辛经历，感受至深，但真要给自己写一段话时，却不知该从何说起。

这几年设计项目一直连续不断，总的来说还算有序，当然有时候也紧张忙乱。但即便是项目扎堆的时候，我对每一个新接的项目也还是会掩不住地兴奋。我喜欢亲自投入到项目设计中，享受创造出美丽空间的成就感。项目着急的时候，就和团队挑灯熬油，一起奋战。得空便整理整理自己的作品，温故知新；同时也看看微刊，了解其他设计师们的新作。闲暇之余，更喜欢出去走走，或是亲近大自然，体味一份放松与安静；或是逛逛市场，邂逅某种新奇与惊喜。

总是很珍惜那些出差、考察和旅行的机会，条件允许时我会精心挑选入住的酒店，因为这是我旅行中极具意义的一部分。最喜欢那些富于设计感的酒店，可能它未必有多豪华，但是很有趣，很有设计感。同时也会担心，怕遇见那种一味堆积材料、豪华而无内涵的酒店，仿佛在大街上看到一个光彩照人的美女，走近了才发现眼窝空洞、了无生趣，原来竟是个全身挂满了珠宝的仿真模特，真是说不出的失落和惋惜。所以我坚信好的设计人人都会喜欢，因为它所呈现的，绝不仅仅是空间，而是一种生活的味道。古典雅致，现代简约，海洋清新，田园闲适，英伦高贵，中式端庄，从一种生活到另一种生活，这就是设计的趣味！这种趣味赋予我源源不断的创作激情，让我在设计创作的伊甸园里，乐此不疲。即便在设计过程中不能做到随心所欲，我也总是会通过不断的变化，做出独特的韵味。

在设计的道路上，其实反反复复地研究推敲，也走过很多曲折的道路。对于设计的理解，随着时间的推移，每个阶段也有所不同。在理想与现实的矛盾面前，单纯追求市场效益，往往意味着对设计理想的妥协。带领着团队，有时候我也会不那么坚持，因为我也认同只有合适才是最好的，符合市场价值观念的设计也是好设计。但赢利只是途径而不是目的，它是我们通往设计理想的漫长道路的基础。妥协也并不意味着放弃，努力地坚持着我们的设计梦想，这既是我的幸福，也是团队的共同凝聚。

感谢一路走来所有客户的认可，因为有你们的信任和支持，我们的设计作品得以最大程度的实现。感谢一路并肩作战的同事，你们的投入、努力、创作的价值得以实现是团队最大的荣耀。感谢家人和朋友们的默默支持、鼓励与包容。可爱的小不丁更给了我无限的幸福感！

Through careful preparation over a year, the new book will be published, the hard experience of this period, feels to the deepest, but to write a paragraph for themselves, but don't know where to start.

There are many designing projects continuously along these years, but on the whole, it is in order, of course, sometimes frantic and busy life. But even when it has the cluster of project, I cannot stop my excitement for the project design. I like to addict myself into the project design, to enjoy the sense of the achievement for creating beautiful space. And when the project was in a hurry, and the team burn boiled together. When I am free, I will tidy up finishing my work, back to refresh an old friend; At the same time, to take a look at the masterpieces of other designers. When it is the leisure time, I prefer to go out for a walk, or make myself closer to the nature, to experience a sense of relaxation and quiet environment; Or around the market, to meet some novelty and surprise.

I always appreciate the opportunities for business trips, visiting and traveling, when conditions permit, I will carefully check the hotel for living, because it is most meaningful part of my journey. Perhaps the most sense of the designed hotel, it is not necessary how luxurious, but very interesting, has a sense of design. At the same time, I am also worried, afraid of meeting te blindly material accumulation is luxurious without the connotation of hotel, as if seeing a radiant and beautiful girl, but when approaching her, discovering that orbital empty barren, turns out a whole body full of jewelry model, really couldn't say regret and sorrow. So I believe that good design which everyone will like it, because it shows, are not just space, but a flavor of life. Classical elegant contemporary and contracted, fresh sea pastoral leisurely, British noble elegant Chinese style, from one kind life to the other kind of life, this is the fun of the design. The interest gives me a steady stream of creative passion, let me lost in the design of the garden of Eden with enthusiasm. Even in the design process, I cannot follow one's inclinations, I also always make use of constant changes, to make a unique flavor.

On the way of design, actually through repeated research, I go through many tortuous path. For the understanding of the design, with the passage of time, each phase is also different. In front of the contradiction between ideal and reality, pure pursuit of market benefit, always means the compromise of the ideal design. Leading the team, sometimes, I think I am not insist, because I believe only the suitable is the best, the market values of design in line with the market are good design. But the profit is a way rather than a purpose, it is the fundamental steps on the long roads to design ideal. Compromise does not mean giving up, trying to stick to our design dreams, this is my happiness, and also the common goal of team cohesion.

Thanks to all the customer recognition along the way, because of your trust and support, we realize our full potential in our designed products. And also thanks to fight alongside colleagues all the way, your input and efforts, the value you create, is the greatest glory for the whole team. Thanks to my family and friends support, encouragement and tolerance. Cute "little Pu-ding" give me infinite happiness.

鄭亮 **Liang Zheng**

我坚信要成为一名合格的设计师，要有强烈的职业道德和社会使命感，要站在客户的立场，用你的专业和智慧使客户利益在有限的预算范围内价值最大化，让设计成为一种有效的生产力。

To be a qualified designer, I firmly believe that we must strong working ethics and sense of social mission, stand for the customers you serve, in order to realize your customers' interest to the fullest with your professionalism and wisdom, so we can turn our design into an effective productivity.

谷衛宁 **Gu Weining**

设计源于生活，生活因设计而改变！让设计融入生活，营造自然、品位、格调；精彩的生活创造出彩的设计效果，用心观察生活，感悟人生真谛，让设计与生活互动，成就空间和谐。

Design comes from life, and like will have change because of design. To make the design concept into life, build the nature, taste and style, wonderful life creates brilliant design effect, observe life carefully, reflect the nature of the true life, to make the interaction between design and life, to achieve the space in harmony. Let the design worthy for something.

丁曉楠 Ding Xiaonan

生命不是用来比较，而是用来完成。所以其实我们更需要的，只是在这个过程里，不断地播种收割自己。虽然有时候这个过程会有些长，可是不要慌，生命没有必要那么分秒必争。觉得乱的时候，就停下来把自己整理清楚。然后再出发。沉住气，忠于内心，生命才饱满。

Life is not to compare, but used to complete. More important for us in the process of life, we need to sow in heart and reap in the harvest. Although sometimes the process maybe feel a little longer, but don't panic, life is not necessary that every minute counts. When something happens disorderly, stop to organize yourself completely. Then start again. Just hold your breath, loyal to your heart, then make the life to the full.

張文 Zhang Wen

设计师的思维是天马行空的，用不同材质不同色彩的饰品打造一个个可以称之为美学的作品。然而设计师的态度是严谨的，不驰于空想，不骛于虚声，惟以求真。

The logic of the designer is unconstrained style, with different colors of jewelry, which are made of different materials, to build up some aesthetic works based on their logic. Although the altitude of the designer is rigorous, however, is not in the tower of Bable, not then to virtual sound, but in truth.

王鑫

Wang Xin

我们的人生何曾不充满梦想，那朵朱槿花儿，就在你我的心灵深处摇摆，那无限的风光我们几欲揽尽。然而我们总是习惯于守候第一个春天，而对第一个季节的空获，我们往往轻率地将第二个春天弃之门外，将梦交归于梦。梦想之花垂青的只是那些有耐心、持着追求的人。今天，倘若给你一朵梦中的朱槿花，你应该有勇气向梦想买断第二个春天。

Our life is full of fantastic dreams, that hibiscus flower, in my heart, the unlimited scenery, we will catch a glimpse of them. But we used to wait for the first season, and tend to rashly get the empty result of the second season, we always put our second dream out of the door, and put the dream to connect that dream. The flower of dream only appreciate those who have patience, constant pursuit of dream. Today, if you are given a hibiscus in a dream, you should have the courage to dream in order to buy a second Spring.

李蕾

Li Lei

把装修好的房子倒过来，这些能掉下来的所有物品，就是软装。软装就像是一串精美首饰，将坚硬的房子与主人的情感相连，用色彩、品位精心装点，组成了这个独一无二的空间。而软装设计师，就是串出这美好的人。

Upside down the decorated house, these items will fall down, that is the soft outfit. Soft outfit is like a string of fine jewelry, connecting the hard house to the master's emotions, with color, taste decorations meticulously, then formed the unique space. And the soft outfit stylist, will string out such a wonderful person.

Tang Wan 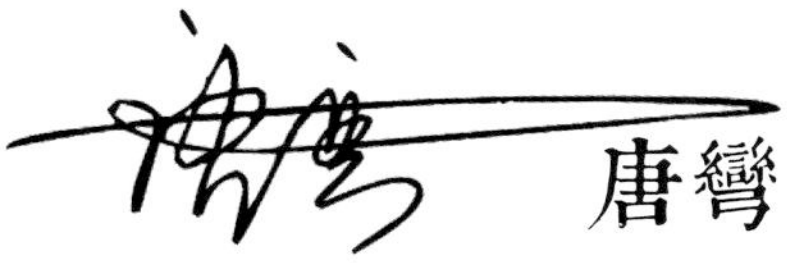 唐彎

每次拿到一个户型，心中便知又是一次激情的交错，这个时刻总是令人兴奋不已。对于设计，自己更看重的是“细节”，“入微的细节带来完美的设计”，对此我是深信的；一个优秀的设计师，定有一颗细腻的心！

When getting a family model, in my heart, a passion of crisscross, this moment is always exciting. To design their value is more "details", more details will bring in perfect design, I am convinced that a brilliant designer, must have a delicate heart.

劉岩

Liu Yan 

由内心去感悟空间，我认为一个空间本有生命，我要做的就是将自己的设计理念赋予其中，赋予其灵魂。到最后，设计成了空间的一部分，让它焕发出不可度量的气质，焕发出活生生的精神。

Feeling from your heart, from my perspective, the space is full of life, for me, I will put my design concept into it, endow them with spirit. At the end of the day, design will be part of the space, let it coruscate gives an measurement of temperament, coruscate gives the dynamic spirit.

汪汝洁 Wang Rujie

当人们的空间被各种物质挤压的时候，也就失去了本质，我们要去掉一切虚假的、表面的、无用的东西，而剩下真实的、本质的、必不可少的东西，因而得到更多的空间、更多的舒适、更多的效率、更多的美……

When the space is pressed by the various substances, it will lose the essence, we need to get rid of all the false, the useless things on the surface, the true and necessary things, so getting more space, more comfortable, more efficient and more beautiful things will occur......

智新 Zhi Xin

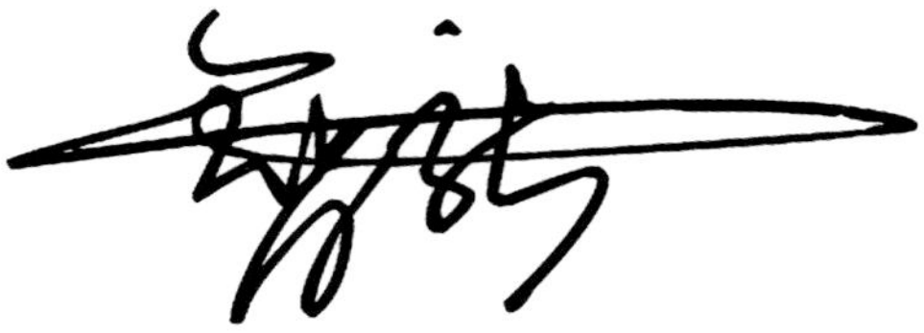

设计是回归本位，点、线、面的灵活运用。力求用一种最简洁最自然的手法来对美进行最为直接的表达。用最少的投入，来最大化地美化和利用现有空间。

Design means returning to the original standard, the flexible use of point, line and surface. Strive to use one of more concise and natural approach to the most direct expression of beauty. With the least amount of inputs, to maximize the beautification and use of existing space.

李丹

Li Dan

其实旅行最大的好处，不是能见到多少人，见过多美的风景，而是走着走着，在一个际遇下，突然重新认识了自己。

Actually the benefit of the traveling, it is not to see many travellers and scenery around you, but along your way, you will update your self-mind based on the new situation.

李琳

Li Lin

人生的所有瓶颈，都如两处悬崖间的渊谷，进退皆可生，只是风景不同罢了。你若放弃那些牵绊，也许另寻蹊径，会随着细水长流到人生平坦之处。你若一门心思想突破悬崖的屏障，也许会由渺小变得强大，拥有向上的力量。

All the bottlenecks of life are like ou deep valley on both sides. Each side, you can enter, the different point is you will experience different view of life. IF you give up those who stumble you, maybe find another way for your remaining life, with the river flowing along the way to the plain life. If you try to break through the cliff barrier, you will probably shift yourself from small to strong, and more importantly, to hold the power for your upward career.

王莹莹
Wang Yingying

我享受一砖一瓦，一草一木，一点一滴，带着诚意做出自己满意的作品。因为它是语言，它是态度，它是追求，更是一颗扑通扑通跳动着的心脏。

I enjoy a brick and a inch, little grass and little tree, a point and a drop, to make satisfactory work with sincerity. Because it is the language, it is attitude. And more importantly, it is a beating and dynamic heart.

陸盛浩
Lu Shenghao

人生是一个不断认识自我、实现自我的过程。是渐渐对别人宽容，反而对自己要求更严苛的过程。慢慢对很多事淡然，反而又对一些事更为坚持。当坚定地决定放弃的时候，往往才是接近成功的开始。

Life is a process of constantly self-understanding, self-realizing process. It is gradually tolerant to others, but more self-control and stringent to ourselves. Gradually, you will regard many things as a regular things, on the contract, you will stick to some issues. When you firmly decided to give up, that is usually close to the beginning of success.

金嵩垒

Jin SongLei

去追求卓越，成功就会出其不意地找上门来。何为大师，何以为大师？我相信人人都可以成为大师，但我也相信能成为大师的都是那些对生活极其严谨的一类人。大师不是自封的，也不是他封的，我们都在成为大师的路上坚定地前行。

To pursue the excellence, success will come to your place unexpectedly. What is a master, how to be a master? I believe that everyone can be a master, but those who are real masters are the category of rigorous people. Master are not self-regarded and self-positioned, and also not his or her calling, we all firmly move the way forward towards masters on the journey of life.

王平平

Wang Pingping

笔下的内容不是来自空想，而是源于对生活的发现，无论设计的东西再华丽，再新颖，再颠覆，都是给人用的。对于工作，我对自己有要求：不可过分依赖电脑技术，切记，你是一名设计师，不是一名电脑修图员；不可一直追随流行设计风格，现在流行的，必是马上过时的；不可因低价商业项目，而放低对作品的要求。

The contents under my writing hands are not from the tower of Babel, but from the discovery towards life, no matter how luxuriant and novel for the design, all are for people. For the work, I have asked to myself, don't rely on the technology, be remember, you are a designer, not a computer repairing figure member; Do not alway follow popular design style, the most popular issues will be outdated, and don't lower the requirement to the work based on the low-priced commercial projects.

李文安

Li Wenan

尽管去开被敲的门，不看一眼，怎么知道门外站着的是不是……如果有人要走进我的生活。那就索性让他进来吧，不好，大不了我再把他轰出去。没必要妄自菲薄，也没必要作茧自缚。

Although knocking at the door, don't catch a glimpse, how to know if anyone or anything stands outside. If someone want to walk into my life, then let him in, if not good, please get him out. No need to look yourself small , no need to look yourself strong as well. Good morning, I can.

王林龍

Wang Linlong

要想做设计，应该先学会做一个真正的人，简单地说如果油、盐、酱、醋放在哪里最合适做饭都不知道，那么你还设计什么。设计应是对生活感受的总结，需要你全身心地去感受它，设计源于生活，也融于生活。

If you want to design something, you should learn to a real person, to be simple, if you do not know where to put the oil, salt, sauce and vinegar, then what you can design. Design should be the author's life experience, to feel it based on your heart, your design should originates from life, and also into life.

姬曼

Ji Man

设计是人运用独创性的高级情感活动，是物质与精神的结合体，她不断地在挖掘我血液里的精神，不断地在超越与探索，在前进与枯死面前，我选择前者，所以必须超越！

Design is the creative and original senior emotion activity, is a combination of matter and spirit, she constantly excavate the spirit in my blood, constantly to cross the cliff and beyond your limit for explore further, in the front of the advancement and death, I definitely choose the former, so I must go beyond.

鄭偉

Zheng Wei

不要以感伤的眼光去看过去，因为过去再也不会回来了，最聪明的办法，就是好好对付你的现在——现在正握在你的手里，你要以堂堂正正的大丈夫气概去迎接如梦如幻的未来。

Don't regard your past with your negative attitude, because past never back again, the smart way towards life is cherish your present which you hold on your hands, you must open your heart and do boldly to meet the dream of the future like the true man.

徐飛

Xu Fei

每一日你所付出的代价都比前一日高，因为你的生命又消短了一天，所以每一日你都要更积极。今天太宝贵，不应该为酸苦的忧虑和辛涩的悔恨所销蚀，抬起下巴，抓住今天，它不再回来。

Every day, you pay higher price for your future, because your short life minus a day. So you should have positive attitude towards life. Today is quite precious, you should not worry about acid concern and regrets, seize each golden minute of the present day, it will no longer come back.

特别致谢

香港置地控股有限公司
隆基泰和实业有限公司
招商局地产控股股份有限公司
北京科技园建设(集团)股份有限公司
北京朝阳大地房地产开发有限公司
润地房地产开发有限公司
金海房地产开发有限公司
万和地产开发有限公司
北京大地海阔房地产开发有限公司
田氏文昊地产集团
盛泰集团
秦新集团
现代建设集团
江河摄影

SPECIAL THANKS

HongKong land holdings co., LTD
Longji Taihe industrial co., LTD
Chinese merchants real estate holdings co., LTD
Beijing science and technology park construction (group) co., LTD
Beijing Chaoyang land real estate development co., LTD
Beijing land real estate development co., LTD
Rundi real estate development co., LTD
Jinhai and Wanhe real estate development co., LTD
Beijing land and vast sea real estate development co., LTD
Tian Shiwen real estate Group
Shengtai Group
Qinxin Group
Modern construction Group

图书在版编目（CIP）数据

地产营销空间 / 张云，张浪，张怀著. -- 北京：
中国轻工业出版社，2014.1
ISBN 978-7-5019-9534-9

Ⅰ. ①地… Ⅱ. ①张… ②张… ③张… Ⅲ. ①房地产
-市场营销学 Ⅳ. ①F293.35

中国版本图书馆 CIP 数据核字 (2013) 第 272507 号

责任编辑　毛旭林　　　责任终审　劳国强
装帧设计　赵　茹　　　责任监印　胡　兵　张　可

出版发行　中国轻工业出版社（北京东长安街 6 号）
邮　　编　100740
印　　刷　北京顺诚彩色印刷有限公司
经　　销　各地新华书店
版　　次　2014 年 1 月第 1 版第 1 次印刷
开　　本　889 × 1194　1/16
印　　张　19
字　　数　210 千字
书　　号　ISBN 978-7-5019-9534-9
定　　价　198.00 元

邮购电话　010-65241695
传　　真　010-65128352
发行电话　010-85119835　85119793
传　　真　010-85113293
网　　址　http://www.chlip.com.cn
E-mail　club@chlip.com.cn
如发现图书残缺请直接与我社邮购联系调换
131220J2X101HBW